FIVE-STAR GIRLS' BASKETBALL DRILLS

Second Edition

Edited by Stephanie V. Gaitley, Leigh Klein and Matt Masiero

Wish Publishing
Terre Haute, Indiana
www.wishpublishing.com

LCCN: 2003101478

Book edited by Stephanie V. Gaitley, Leigh Klein and Matt Masiero
Proofread by Natalie Chambers
Cover designed by Phil Velikan
Diagrams by Debbie Oldenburg

Printed in the United States of America
10 9 8 7 6 5 4 3 2

Published in the United States by
Wish Publishing
P.O. Box 10337
Terre Haute, IN 47801, USA
www.wishpublishing.com

Distributed in the United States by
Cardinal Publishers Group
Indianapolis, Indiana 46264

CONTENTS

Acknowledgments

Dear Coaches,

   I want to thank everyone who participated in making this book come to life. The women's game will continue to grow because of our commitment to helping aspiring coaches learn more about the game through each other.

   Thanks for taking the time out of your busy schedules to add your favorite drill or skill. I'm sure some young coaches will make great use of your information.

Best wishes for much continued success.

Sincerely,
Stephanie V. Gaitley
Women's Basketball Coach, Long Island University

Introduction

Twenty years ago, Rick Pitino and Kathy Delaney-Smith put the idea of serious girls' basketball instruction the Five-Star way to work with the first-ever Five-Star Women's Camp at Boston University. Since that time, Five-Star has worked tirelessly to continue that idea with camps in seven states and clinics with the Turkish Basketball Federation that featured Wendy Larry of Old Dominion (1997) and Stephanie V. Gaitley of Long Island University (1996). This book is a natural outgrowth of this philosophy.

Several thousand players have convened on our courts to take their game to the next level, whether that be making their high school team or playing in the WNBA. Players at every level of play can utilize the drills and philosophies found in this book. This book emphasizes what we teach at the Five-Star Camps: Success comes from the individual, her practice technique, her progressive goal planning and the intensity she brings to the court. With these three elements and a variety of creative drills for skill development, each player can become the best player she can be.

When *Five-Star Basketball Drills* was originally published in 1988, little did we know it was going to become the best-selling basketball drill book and inspire so many great players. To illustrate that point, when Trajan Langdon (currently of the Cleveland Cavaliers) was a senior in high school, he was asked how he had become such a great player. Trajan replied that he had studied a great deal of game tapes and that when he was a youth, his father had bought him a copy of the Five-Star drill book. He was so inspired that he used the book to practice two to three hours a day. We would like this book — filled with the best drills from today's top students of the game — to have the same influence on you, our reader, that the original *Five-Star Drills* had on Trajan and fill you with the determination and drill work you'll need to elevate your game.

We wish you the greatest success in your quest to achieve your potential.

Leigh Klein,
President of Five-Star International Basketball Camps

Matt Masiero,
Director, Five-Star Women's Camp

CHAPTER ONE
Strength Training, Conditioning and Nutrition

Matt Brzycki, Coordinator of Health Fitness,
Strength and Conditioning Programs
Princeton University
Princeton, New Jersey

Strength & Conditioning

A strength-and-conditioning program is vital in preparing your athletes for the physical demands of basketball. There is, however, a wide range of programs from which to choose as well as considerable debate as to which one is most appropriate. As coaches, you are well aware that time is a precious commodity. Because of this, you should seek and implement a strength-and-conditioning program that produces the *maximum* results in the *minimum* amount of time. As such, efficiency should be the major consideration in selecting your program. By utilizing a program that is time-efficient, your athletes will have more time available to pursue other activities such as perfecting their basketball skills and preparing for academic experiences. Your players should *invest* time in a strength-and-conditioning program, not *spend* time.

STRENGTH TRAINING

The main purpose of strength training is to prevent injury. According to data collected for the NCAA Injury Surveillance System, the top two body parts that are most frequently injured in women's college basketball — in practices as well as games — have historically been the ankle and knee. Of particular concern are injuries to the anterior cruciate ligament (ACL) which occur in women basketball players seven times more frequently in practices and five times more frequently in games than in their male counterparts. Increasing the strength of your players' muscles, bones and connective tissue will allow them to tolerate stresses that might otherwise cause an injury.

A second purpose of strength training is to increase your players' performance potential. Strength training will not automatically make your athletes into better players but it will improve their *potential* to be better

2

players. They must still learn how to apply their increased strength on the basketball court.

Interestingly, science has been unable to determine that one strength-training method is superior to another. Research has only shown that a variety of methods can increase strength. For example, one study found no statistically significant differences in the strength increases produced by nine different training routines consisting of various combinations of sets and repetitions. It has also been shown — both scientifically and empirically — that strength can be improved with a variety of equipment, including barbells, dumbbells and machines.

So, just about any type of strength-training program has the potential to produce favorable results. However, many methods of strength training are more favorable than others. For example, your strength-training program should be practical in the sense that it is relatively easy for you and your athletes to understand. In some instances, strength-training programs have become grossly overcomplicated and correspondingly confusing. The use of pseudoscientific terminology coupled with pre-planned programs that specify inflexible instructions to vary the sets, repetitions, intensity and volume of activity in rigidly defined "phases" of periodization adds to the confusion. Remember, too, that references to the training methodology of Eastern European weightlifters are irrelevant and, therefore, do not apply to your basketball players — unless your basketball players are also competitive weightlifters. And, of course, efficiency should be a major consideration.

A practical and efficient strength-training program can be designed — using virtually any type of equipment — by applying the following concepts:

Intensity

An athlete's level of intensity (or effort) is the most important factor in an efficient strength-training program. Essentially, the greater the intensity, the better the response. In the weight room, a high level of intensity is characterized by performing each exercise to the point of muscular fatigue: when an athlete has exhausted her muscles to the extent that she literally cannot perform any more repetitions. Failure to reach a desirable level of muscular fatigue — or effort — will result in submaximal gains in muscular strength.

Evidence for this "threshold" is suggested in the literature by the "overload principle" that was proven experimentally in the 1950s. The overload principle states that in order to increase muscular strength, a muscle must be stressed — or "overloaded" — with a workload that is beyond its present capacity. The effort must be great enough to exceed this threshold so that a sufficient amount of muscular fatigue is produced to trigger an increase in muscular strength. Simply, exercise that does not produce enough muscular fatigue will not stimulate muscular strength.

Progression

The term "progressive resistance exercise" was coined in the 1940s. Unfortunately, little of what is done in most weight rooms today can be considered "progressive." Suppose that one of your athletes did a set of leg curls for 10 repetitions with 100 pounds and a month later she is still doing 10 repetitions with 100 pounds. Did she increase her strength? Probably not. On the other hand, what if she was able to do 11 repetitions with 120 pounds a month later? In this case, she performed 10 percent more repetitions with 20 percent more weight.

If a muscle is to continually improve in strength it must be forced to do progressively harder work. Muscles must be overloaded with a workload that is increased steadily and systematically throughout the course of a strength-training program.

The application of progression does not have to be as complex nor as restrictive as a periodization program. In order to overload her muscles, an athlete must attempt to increase either the weight that she used or the repetitions that she performed in relation to her previous workout. Each time an athlete achieves the maximum number of prescribed repetitions in an exercise, she should increase the resistance in that exercise for her next workout. The increase in resistance should be made in an amount with which each athlete is comfortable. Muscles will respond better if the progressions in resistance are five percent or less. But again, remember that the resistance must always be challenging.

If an athlete cannot do the maximum number of prescribed repetitions in an exercise, she should use the same resistance in that exercise for her next workout and try to perform a greater number of repetitions.

Sets

One of the most controversial areas in strength training concerns the number of sets that should be done for each exercise. For decades, it was generally accepted that performing multiple sets of an exercise was better than single sets. In 1998, Dr. Ralph Carpinelli and Dr. Robert Otto of Adelphi University (New York) destroyed this belief with an astonishing discovery. Their comprehensive literature review of all relevant research that examined different numbers of sets — 35 studies which dated back to 1956 — showed that there were no significant differences between single- and multiple-set training in all but two studies. In a later review, Dr. Carpinelli noted two additional studies that found no significant differences between single- and multiple-set training.

Besides the compelling scientific evidence, the fact of the matter is that performing one set to muscular fatigue is a very popular method of strength training. Indeed, single-set training is advocated by numerous strength-and-conditioning coaches at all levels of competition, including high school, college and professional.

If one set of each exercise produces the same results as two or three sets, then a one-set protocol represents a more efficient means of strength training. After all, why have your athletes perform several sets when they can obtain similar results from one set in a fraction of the time? This is not to say that traditional multiple-set programs are unproductive. It is just that multiple sets are extremely inefficient in terms of time and, therefore, are undesirable for your athletes.

Of course, if a single set of an exercise is to be productive, your players must do each exercise with an appropriate level of intensity — that is, to the point of muscular fatigue. Their muscle(s) must be completely fatigued at the end of each exercise.

Repetitions

In order to produce an increase in strength, a muscle must be exercised for an appropriate amount of time. Because it is characterized by short-term, high-intensity efforts, strength training is considered to be an anaerobic endeavor. Optimal time frames in the anaerobic domain are about 90 – 120 seconds for the buttocks, 60 – 90 seconds for the legs and 40 – 70 seconds for the upper torso.

This information can be used to formulate repetition ranges. For example, if a weight is raised in about two seconds and lowered in about four seconds, each repetition would be about six seconds long. Considering the aforementioned time frames and six-second repetitions yields the following repetition ranges: 15 – 20 for exercises involving the buttocks, 10 – 15 for the legs and 6 – 12 for the upper torso.

It should be noted that having your players attempt one-repetition maximums or perform low-repetition movements that are considerably less than the optimal time frames will increase their risk of injury. Likewise, as they exercise beyond the recommended time frames, it becomes a greater test of their aerobic endurance rather than anaerobic strength.

According to most authorities, strength training should not be done until the age of about 13 or 14. At this young age, it is safer to perform more repetitions than previously suggested in order to reduce orthopedic stress. The higher repetitions will necessitate using lighter weights that will, in turn, reduce the stress placed upon their bones and joints. For example, younger teenagers might use the following repetition ranges: 20 – 25 for exercises involving the buttocks, 15 – 20 for the legs and 10 – 15 for the upper torso.

Technique

Your athletes should raise the weight in a deliberate, controlled manner without any jerking movements. In general, they should raise the weight in about 1 – 2 seconds. Raising the weight in a rapid, explosive fashion is not recommended for two reasons. First, it increases the involvement of momentum thereby making the exercise less productive and less efficient; second, it exposes the muscles, joints and connective tissue to potentially dangerous forces which magnify the likelihood of incurring an injury while strength training.

After raising the weight, your athletes should pause briefly in the position of full muscular contraction, or the "mid-range" position. Pausing momentarily in this position emphasizes their muscles when they are fully contracted. Further, a brief pause in the mid-range position permits a smooth transition between the raising and the lowering of the weight and helps reduce the adverse effects of momentum.

In order to attain optimal results from strength training, your athletes must emphasize the lowering of the weight. In general, they should lower the weight in about 3 – 4 seconds. Emphasizing the lowering of the weight makes the exercise more efficient: The same muscles that are used to raise the weight are also used to lower it. Therefore, each repetition becomes more efficient and each set becomes more productive.

In effect, each repetition should be roughly 4 – 6 seconds in length. A 16-week study demonstrated a 50 percent increase in upper-body strength and a 33 percent increase in lower-body strength in a group that performed each repetition by raising the weight in two seconds and lowering the weight in four seconds.

Finally, your athletes should perform each repetition throughout the greatest possible range of motion (ROM) that safety allows. Exercising throughout a full ROM will allow them to maintain — or perhaps increase — their flexibility. Furthermore, this ensures that the entire target muscle is being exercised — not just a portion of it — thereby making the movement more efficient. In other words, full-range exercise is necessary for a full-range effect.

Duration

More is not necessarily better when it comes to strength training (or conditioning, for that matter). Common sense suggests that as your athletes increase the length of their activity, they must decrease the level of their effort. Stated otherwise, your athletes cannot exercise with a high level of effort for long periods of time. Carbohydrates are the body's preferred source of energy during intense exercise. Most people exhaust their carbohydrate stores after about one hour of intense exercise. Therefore, strength workouts should be completed in no more than one hour — and even less when in-season.

Your athletes should take a minimum amount of recovery between exercises. The length of their recovery interval depends upon their present level of fitness. Initially, your athletes may require a recovery time of about three minutes between efforts; with improved fitness, their pace should quicken to the point where they are moving as rapidly as possible between exercises. (The speed with which they perform their repetitions should not be quickened — just the pace between exercises.)

Volume

A strength-training program must address all of the major muscle groups in the body — not just the "showy" ones. Frequently, muscles that are injured while playing basketball get ignored (such as those surrounding the knee) while muscles that are more cosmetic than anything else get highlighted (such as the abdominals).

A comprehensive strength-training program for basketball can be performed using no more than 15 exercises during each total-body workout. The focal point for most of these exercises should be their hips, legs and upper torso. Specifically, one exercise should be included for their hips, hamstrings, quadriceps, calves/dorsi flexors, biceps, triceps, forearms, abdominals and lower back. Because the shoulder joint allows movement at many different angles, two exercises should be selected for their chest, upper back ("lats") and shoulders.

There is nothing wrong with having your athletes perform more movements than this in order to emphasize a particular body part. As long as they continue to make improvements in their strength, they are not doing too many exercises. However, if their strength begins to level off or "plateau" in one or more exercises, it is probably because they are overtraining. Along these lines, the volume of exercises should be reduced during the season.

Sequence

A strength-training program should begin with exercises that influence the largest muscles and proceed to those that involve the smallest muscles. Have your athletes perform exercises for their hips first, followed by their upper legs (hamstrings and quadriceps), lower legs (calves or dorsi flexors), upper torso (chest, upper back and shoulders), arms (biceps, triceps and forearms), abdominals and finally their lower back.

It is important that your athletes do not fatigue their midsection early in their workouts. The abdominals stabilize the rib cage and aid in forced expiration during intense activity. Therefore, early fatigue of their abdominals would detract from their performance in other exercises that involve their larger, more powerful muscles.

Frequency

Intense strength training places great demands on the muscular system. In order to adapt to those demands, your athletes must receive an adequate amount of recovery between strength workouts. Muscles do not get stronger during a workout — muscles get stronger during the recovery from a workout. When weights are lifted, muscle tissue is broken down and the recovery process allows the muscle time to rebuild itself. Think of this as allowing a wound to heal. If you had a scab and picked at it every day, you would delay the healing process. But if you left it alone, you would permit the damaged tissue time to heal. There are individual variations in recovery ability — everyone has different levels of tolerance for exercise. However, a period of about 48 – 72 hours is usually necessary for muscle tissue to recover sufficiently from an intense strength-training workout.

Adequate recovery is also required to return carbohydrate stores to their preexercise levels. Because approximately 48 hours are needed to replenish depleted carbohydrate stores following intense physical activity, it is suggested that your athletes perform their strength training 2 – 3 times per week on nonconsecutive days — such as on Monday, Wednesday and Friday.

Keep in mind that a strength-training program should be done year-round — including the basketball season. Remember, it is during the competitive season that your players need to be at their best in terms of strength (and conditioning). To provide adequate recovery, however, the frequency of their strength training should be reduced to 1 – 2 times per week when in-season.

Documentation

The importance of accurate record keeping cannot be overemphasized. Records are a log of what your athletes accomplish during each and every exercise of each and every workout.

A workout card can be an extremely valuable tool for you to monitor the progress of your athletes and make their workouts more meaningful. It can also be used to identify exercises in which an athlete has reached a plateau. In the unfortunate event that an athlete incurs an injury, the effectiveness of the rehabilitative process can be gauged if there is a record of her preinjury strength levels.

A workout card can take an infinite number of appearances. However, your athletes should be able to record their body weight, the date of each workout, the weight used for each exercise, the number of repetitions performed for each exercise and the order in which the exercises were completed. The recommended repetition ranges should also be given for each exercise along with spaces to record any seat adjustments.

CONDITIONING

In order for your basketball players to compete at their full potential, it is also important for them to be as highly conditioned as possible. Basketball — like most team sports — has an *anaerobic* element since it primarily consists of a series of short-term, high-intensity efforts. However, basketball also has an *aerobic* (or endurance) element since these anaerobic efforts are required over a fairly lengthy period of time. Conditioning for basketball, therefore, must involve aerobic and anaerobic efforts.

Similar to strength training, conditioning can be improved using a wide variety of equipment, including stationary bicycles, rowers and stairclimbers. Because basketball is a sport in which your athletes must run, most of their conditioning work should be accomplished by running. If you have heavier athletes, however, it is a good idea for them to do at least some of their conditioning with low-impact, nonweight-bearing activities — such as pedaling stationary bicycles — to reduce the potential for orthopedic problems that can result from the high-impact forces of running.

You can design a practical and efficient conditioning program for your athletes by incorporating the following concepts:

Frequency

When not in-season, your players should do conditioning workouts three times per week on nonconsecutive days. It is critical to first establish a solid foundation of aerobic support. In the early off-season, then, these three workouts should be aerobic in nature — that is, they should consist of continuous, long-term efforts.

In the middle of the off-season, you should reduce the frequency of their aerobic workouts to twice a week and add an anaerobic workout in its place — such as interval training that involves repeated bouts of short-term, high-intensity efforts alternated with periods of recovery. At this point in the off-season, each of these efforts (sprints) should last about 1½ – 3 minutes. As an example, you might have your athletes run a series of four half-mile intervals with a goal of three minutes per interval.

By the end of the off-season, you should decrease their aerobic workouts to once a week and increase their anaerobic workouts to twice a week. At this point in the off-season, one of their anaerobic workouts should involve a series of longer efforts of 1½ – 3 minutes and a series of shorter efforts of less than 90 seconds.

During the preseason and in-season, most of your team's conditioning work can be done during practice. You can also have your players do different sprint drills at the end of practice.

Duration

Similar to strength training, more is not necessarily better when it comes to conditioning. Excluding a warm-up, conditioning workouts — whether they are aerobic or anaerobic — need not exceed 30 minutes. In fact, some conditioning workouts can be completed in as little as 18 – 20 minutes. Keep in mind, however, that although the length of the workout is low, the intensity of the effort that would be expected of your players is quite high.

Progression

Like strength training, it is important that conditioning be progressively more challenging. In general, there are three ways that your players can provide progression from one conditioning workout to the next. One way is to cover the same distance at a faster pace — that is, in a shorter amount of time. A second way is to cover a greater distance at the same pace. A third way is to increase both the distance and the pace.

In an aerobic workout in the early off-season, for example, you might require your players to run 3 miles in 24 minutes. To make the next aerobic workout more demanding, they could run 3 miles in 23:55, run 3.05 miles in 24:00 or 3.05 miles in 23:55. Anaerobic workouts should also be made progressively more challenging using similar methods.

YOUR DECISION

Coaches and players are quick to jump on the bandwagon of successful teams. In most cases, you will find that many teams are successful in basketball despite the fact that they use vastly different strength-and-conditioning programs. So, how do you decide on which program to administer to your players? When you consider a strength-and-conditioning program, ask yourself the following five questions:

Is it productive?

Is it comprehensive?

Is it practical?

Is it efficient?
Is it safe?

If the answer to any one of these five questions is "no," then the program is not in the best interests of you or your players. Expressed in different terms, you should select and implement a program that is productive, comprehensive, practical, efficient and safe.

NOTE: This chapter represents a thumbnail overview of strength and conditioning for basketball. A more detailed description can be found in the book *Conditioning for Basketball* written by Matt Brzycki and Shaun Brown (the strength and conditioning coach of the Boston Celtics).

Debra Wein, M.S., R.D.
President and Co-Founder,
The Sensible Nutrition Connection
www.sensiblenutrition.com

Nutrition for Peak Performance

The body requires over 40 fundamental nutrients to maintain good health. To get all these nutrients and nonnutrient compounds important for health, it is best to eat a variety of foods from all food groups. No one food can supply your body with all the nutrients you need. Eating a diet that includes many different foods ensures you will get more of the vitamins, minerals and other substances your body needs to function its best and fight off disease. While some people think they can take a supplement to make up for a poor diet, many more substances in food are being discovered that may protect health and prevent disease. Therefore, be sure to include foods that contain all of the nuts and bolts your body needs for optimal health.

Have you ever wondered?

♦ What do fruits and vegetables have that milk doesn't?

♦ What's in lean meats that is not in pasta?

♦ What do the nutrients in the foods we eat every day do for us?

Check out the table on the following page to find out answers to these and other interesting questions.

Nutrient	Food Sources	What is it for?	How much do we need?
Carbohydrates	Breads, pasta, cereal, rice, grains, fruits, vegetables	Fuels the brain and muscles. The primary energy source for moderate-to-high intensity exercise.	55-65% of total calories. The major source of calories in the diet.
Protein	meat, fish, eggs, poultry, beans, legumes, dairy	Essential for building and repairing every cell in the body. Not an optimal energy souce for exercise.	15-20% of total calories. Requirements are easily met through food sources.
Fat	butter, oils, lard, margarine, salad dressing, fried foods, mayo, shortening	Provides insulation and protection. The primary source of stored energy. Used for low-to-moderate intensity exercise. Source of essential fatty acids.	20-30% of total calories. Most people get more than they need. Fat should be limited in individuals trying to lose weight.
Vitamins: water soluble & fat soluble	Eating a wide variety of foods will help you meet the RDA (recommended daily allowance) for each vitamin	Metabolic *catalysts* that regulate reactions in the body. Your body cannot manufacture them - they must be obtained from food.	An RDA has been set for each essential vitamin at a safe and adequate level. RDAs are based on sex and age.

Nutrient	Food Sources	What is it for?	How much do we need?
Minerals	Eating a wide variety of foods will help you meet the RDA for each mineral	Elements combine to form structures of the body. Regulates body processes. Your body cannot manufacture them — they must be obtained from food.	An RDA has been set for most essential minerals at a safe and adequate level.
Water	Beverages, fruits and vegetables	Essential substance making up 50-55% of your body weight. Transports nutrients and wastes in the body. Necessary for proper cell function.	Adequate amounts are necessary to replace daily loses.
Phytochemicals	Plant foods, especially fruits and vegetables	Nonnutrient substances which impart protective benefits to health. May be important for reducing risk of cancer, heart disease, diabetes, cataracts & macular degeneration.	Choosing a minimun of five servings of fruits and vegetables daily may help reduce risk of many chronic diesases.

IDENTIFY AREAS OF IMPORTANCE IN THE DIET

When examining your dietary intake, there are several areas of concern: quantity of food, quality of food, frequency of intake and dietary behaviors. Although it is difficult to assess all areas at once, understanding the interaction between the areas over time will help you choose a diet:

1) Specific to your needs
2) Achievable for you
3) Compatible with the your lifestyle
4) Sustainable over the longterm

Quantity of food

Clearly overall calories are an important element. An estimate of the daily energy intake will allow for comparisons with daily energy expenditure and appropriate weight loss, gain or maintenance. Moderate increases or decreases in daily intake, or levels of exercise over a period of time will produce permanent results — not drastic changes in calories.

Quality of food

Be sure to include regular and daily intake from all of the food groups. Consume a regular intake of bread, cereal, rice, pasta, fruit, vegetable, protein (fish, poultry, meat, legumes, soy products) and dairy.

Include a variety of:

♦ Bread and cereal — wheat, oat, multigrain, high fiber
♦ Rice — Brown, wild, basmati
♦ Pasta — whole wheat, spinach, various shapes and sizes
♦ Fruit — citrus, apples, pears, bananas, berries, melons
♦ Vegetable — cruciferous (broccoli, cauliflower, cabbage), dark leafy greens, squash, tomatoes, carrots
♦ Dairy — low-fat milk, yogurt, cheese

Choose fresh food

Processed foods are generally high in sodium and contain additives and preservatives, damaging flavor and nutrient content. Recently, new nutrients, termed *phytochemicals* (phyto meaning plants) were discovered in foods that provide our bodies with disease-preventing nutrients.

Nutritional supplements continue to be very popular for a variety of reasons — their promise to provide things such as boosts in energy, weight loss or increased performance. Take a look at the food you are eating versus the supplements you are taking. Are the supplements adding nutrients that otherwise would not be there or are they just adding excess energy to a diet that would benefit from a basic nutritional shape-up? A multi-vitamin/multi-mineral if you are trying to lose weight and extra carbs and adequate protein if you are in training are examples of beneficial supplementation; however, more often than not, supplementing to excess is the case. Sorting through the hype will save you effort and money.

Frequency of intake

1. Are your calories spread equally over the course of the day? A lot of people tend to eat light during the day and overeat at night. Starving during the day causes a drop in energy, often resulting in a search for a high-sugar snack. What you really need is to fuel your body over the day, especially if you are active. The need to eat a lot at night will inevitably diminish over time.

2. Is snacking being used healthfully or as a desperate attempt to get energy? Snacking can be the healthiest thing you do. Snacks can fill in the nutrient gaps in the overall diet. For example, if you rarely have milk or cheese in your meals and seem to be lacking dairy, try snacking on yogurt, frozen yogurt or pudding (made with low-fat milk).

3. Are you a weekend eater? When the intake is "good" Monday through Friday afternoon and significantly different from Friday evening to Sunday, accomplishing goals is difficult. This is often a sign of severe restriction during the week that is leading to weekend binges.

Dietary behaviors

1. Do you eat in response to moods?
2. Which moods — anger, frustration, depression or happiness?
3. Do you eat more when you are alone? When you are with others?
4. Do you plan ahead?

5. Are you in control of your environment or are you letting your environment control you?

Identifying negative behaviors is a good beginning, but it requires a lot of work and support to overcome them. Get additional help from a registered dietician and share your own experiences, if appropriate.

You Can Have A Busy Life And A Healthy Diet!

Do you feel like you are so busy that you barely have time to sleep, let alone eat healthy and exercise? We could all use an extra two (or more) hours in the day. Even though we know that fueling our bodies with healthy foods is very important, often our "life" gets in the way.

Does this sound familiar?

I'll start eating better ...

... Next Monday

... After the big deadline

... When school is over

... When I have more time

... After the holidays

You barely have time to eat anything let alone think about eating healthy. Grocery shopping and preparing meals are often out of the question. The fact is that if you can't find the time ... you MAKE the time! Your body will thank you in the long run! Contrary to popular belief (or popular excuses) eating a healthy diet is not "hard work." Like anything else, it just takes knowledge and practice. Below are some strategies to get you started. Remember, eating healthy is not all-or-nothing. Every positive change helps.

Suggestions For Fitting It All In When You Are On The Go

Plan. Plan what, when, where, and how. Schedule time to eat, just like you schedule a meeting. Busy lives mean planning and compromising. You can compromise on time without compromising on nutritional quality. Plan breakfast meetings, and develop a list of lunches and snacks you can eat at your desk or while you are on the go.

Eat a variety of foods that you like. Eating many different foods ensures that you get all the nutrients (and nonnutrient compounds) you need for optimal health without getting too many of the things that may not be as nutritious. Choosing a variety of foods also prevents boredom and increases the number of foods for you to choose from.

Snack. Snacking is also a great way to "take 5" and relieve stress. Always have nutritious snacks on hand to munch on. Choose nutrient- dense foods to fill in the gaps in your diet. If, for example, you have difficulty meeting your daily calcium requirements, choose yogurt, pudding, low-fat cheese or low-fat milk for snacking. Snacking helps you re-fuel and prevents you from becoming so hungry you overeat.

Be an educated eater. Learn the basics of good nutrition, label reading, and dining out. Being an educated eater means you have the knowledge necessary to make informed choices no matter how crunched for time you become.

Shop the perimeter of the grocery store. Think about where all the fresh food is usually located. Push your cart in a big circle and you will end up with a basket full of fresh fruits and vegetables, just-baked whole-grain breads, low-fat dairy products, lean meats, poultry and fish. Go to the middle aisles for staples only. You'll save time and money.

Don't skip meals. Skipping meals not only causes you to miss nutrients important for you health and performance (mental and physical), it also can lead to overeating. You become so hungry that "anything goes" (into your mouth) and all good intentions go out the window. Oftentimes you end up eating the first thing you can grab that may — or more likely may not — be nutritious, and lots of it.

Be creative. Think of time-saving eating opportunities such as eating while commuting, lunches you can eat at your desk, and dinners you can fix in 10 minutes or less. Keep in mind, dinner doesn't have to be hot to be nutritious and breakfast can be leftovers from a previous meal. Well-planned snacks can provide you with an opportunity to refuel and meet your nutritional requirements.

Be flexible. Things don't always work out the way we planned. Be prepared and have an alternative (or two). Don't give up or give in. Make the best of bad situations

Remember, you can fit good nutrition into a busy lifestyle if you ...

♦ Make the commitment to your health
♦ Strive for improvements one at a time
♦ Set weekly goals
♦ Monitor your progress
♦ Reward your successes

♦ Be good to yourself
♦ Make healthy lifestyle changes
♦ Make the time

Depending on the duration, intensity and type of exercise you are performing, there are three stages where nutrition plays a role in performance — before, during and after activity. The goals of carbohydrate and fluid nutrition strategies are to optimize the availability of muscle glycogen and to keep the body well hydrated, thereby insuring optimal performance.

PREEXERCISE NUTRITION

Properly nourishing yourself before exercise should:
♦ Prevent low blood sugar during exercise
♦ Provide fuel by topping off your muscle glycogen stores
♦ Settle your stomach, absorb gastric juices and prevent hunger
♦ Instill confidence in your abilities

Remember, fasting is detrimental to performance and is strongly discouraged before exercise or performance.

The preexercise meal should consist primarily of high-carbohydrate, low-fat foods for easy and fast digestion. Since everyone's preferences for and responses to different foods are unique, it is recommended that you learn through trial and error what works and does not work for your own body. For example, some people respond negatively to sugar intake within an hour before exercise. The temporary "boost" that some people experience after eating foods with a high sugar (sucrose) concentration such as candy, syrups or soft drinks actually causes an increase in insulin production that will be followed by a rapid lowering of blood sugar and can lead to decreased performance. In addition, fructose (the sugar present in fruit juices) ingested before exercise may also lower your blood sugar and cause gastrointestinal distress in many people.

Allow adequate time for digestion and normalization of blood glucose:
♦ 4 hours for a large meal
♦ 2 – 3 hours for a smaller meal
♦ 1 hour for a blended meal, a high carbohydrate beverage (10-30%), or a small snack

For an early morning event, plan wisely so that you can consume at least a smaller meal 2-3 hours before race time. If you know you get nervous or jittery and lose your appetite before an event, make a special effort to eat well the day before. Always eat familiar foods before a competition, don't try anything new and risk affecting your performance. Experiment only during your training.

Foods high in carbohydrates include: fruits, cereal, pasta, breads, rice and other grains.

During exercise

When you eat a diet that is already high in carbohydrates, 60% or greater, there is enough energy in the muscles to fuel workouts and other activities completed within 90 – 120 minutes. On the other hand, during prolonged, strenuous exercise lasting over 2 hours, carbohydrate ingestion at regular intervals during the exercise is beneficial. For example, consuming 8 ounces (1 cup) of a sport drink containing a 6 – 10 % carbohydrate concentration every 15 – 20 minutes can delay the onset of fatigue. This is equivalent to a rate of .8 – 1.0 grams of carbohydrate per minute or approximately 24 – 30 grams every half hour.

Postexercise nutrition

When and what you eat after a workout can have a serious effect on your recovery. Adequate recovery means that your muscles are rested, refueled and ready to perform again, which is extremely important for people who exercise every day. Inadequate recovery can lead to chronic fatigue and a gradual decline in your performance. Be selective in what you eat after exercise; wise choices will help you recover quickly and enable your muscles to work better the next time around. For the fitness enthusiast whose workouts generally last less than 90 minutes, your main concern is to refuel with a well-balanced, high-carbohydrate diet. However, if your workouts typically last longer than 90 minutes and are "exhaustive," the timing of your meals is additionally important. Your body needs about 20 hours to replenish its fuel stores. Furthermore, this will only occur if adequate carbohydrates (approximately 500-600 grams depending on your body size) are consumed during this time. The first 2 – 3 hours after exercise are critical for you; don't wait to eat.

For optimal glycogen resynthesis follow these target intakes during the 20 hours following a workout:

- Immediately after exercise (15-30 minutes): 75 – 100 grams carbohydrate
- Within the next 2 – 3 hours after exercise: 100 grams carbohydrate
- Every 4 hours thereafter: 100 grams carbohydrate

For example, since 1 gram carbohydrate = 4 calories, 75 – 100 grams = 300 - 400 calories. In practical terms, you could take in 75 – 100 grams of carbohydrate by eating:

- A banana and a bagel
- ½ cup raisins and a slice of bread
- 2 cups of orange juice and a cup of yogurt.

A high-carbohydrate beverage (10 – 30% carbohydrate concentration) can also be used as an immediate source of carbohydrate replenishment. These beverages can be especially useful after a workout in the heat when you may be more inclined to drink than to eat. However, high carbohydrate beverages are not complete foods; they do not contain all the nutrients your body needs for good health and top performance. If you use these beverages in your training regimen, make sure you follow soon after with a well-balanced, high-carbohydrate meal and plenty of fluids.

FLUID AND HYDRATION GUIDELINES

Water is an essential nutrient making up 50 – 55% of your weight. Water cools your body. As you exercise your body temperature increases and you sweat. As the sweat evaporates from your skin, you cool down. Dehydration will occur if the body water you lose is not replaced. You can become dehydrated even when you lose just a few pounds of water as sweat. Dehydration can be dangerous resulting in chills, clammy skin, throbbing heartbeat, nausea and decreased performance. Here's what you need to know to avoid dehydration.

Before exercise: *Hyper-hydrate*

Drink before exercise! 1 – 2 hours before exercise drink 2½ cups (20 oz.) of water.

15 – 30 minutes before exercise drink another 1½ cups (12 oz.) of water for a total of 4 cups (32 oz.).

During exercise: *Hydrate*

Drink 1 cup (8 oz.) of water or sport drink every 15 – 20 minutes during a workout.

After exercise: *Rehydrate*

Weigh yourself before and after a workout. For each pound of body weight lost drink 2 cups (16 oz.) of water or sport drink. If you don't have access to a scale, drink until your urine is clear. Clear urine is a good indication of adequate hydration.

Other tips to keep you performing at your best:

♦ Drink before you're thirsty since thirst is not always a good indicator of fluid loss.

♦ Avoid caffeine and alcohol, they increase fluid losses.

♦ Drink fluids at a cool temperature.

♦ Unless you are an ultraendurance athlete participating in events lasting over 8 hours, electrolyte (sodium, potassium, and chloride) losses from exercise are easily overcome by typical intakes from the regular diet. Therefore, salt tablets and other electrolyte replacements are not recommended.

Coach Cheryl Dozier
University at Buffalo, SUNY
Buffalo, New York

10 Seconds

Purpose:
To improve transition, running the floor and conditioning skills.

Organization:
This drill requires three players.

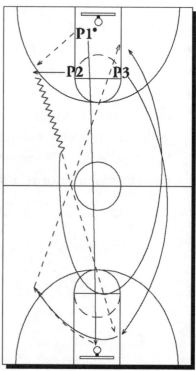

1) The drill begins with three players standing in the lane. Player 1 has the ball in front of the basket and the other two are at the elbows with at least one foot inside the paint.

2) Player 1 throws the ball off the glass, rebounds it, and outlets it to one of the other players who has gone to the outlet positions as the ball hits the glass.

3) The player who catches the outlet is to push the ball up the middle of the floor.

4) The player who does not receive the outlet will sprint up the floor and receive the long pass from the wing with the ball for a lay-up.

5) After passing for the lay-up, the player who makes the pass (player 2 in the diagram) has to touch one foot in the paint and sprint back the other way, this time to be the player who receives the pass and shoots the lay-up.

6) Player 1's job is to simply sprint the floor, take the ball out of the net, and outlet it to the player who hit the lay-up (player 3 in the diagram).

7) Player 3, after she makes her lay-up, sprints to the outlet position and will throw the long pass to player 1.

8) Not only must the two lay-ups be made in the allotted 10 seconds, but all three players must have a foot in the paint before 10 seconds are up as well.

Coach Matt Masiero
Director, Five-Star Basketball Camp
Yonkers, New York

Agility Series

Purpose:
To improve footwork, quickness and agility.

Organization:
Each drill is done at full speed to maximize the benefits and simulate game conditioning.

Line Series
Each drill is done in 15-second intervals up to 1 minute.
For example: first set is 15 seconds, second set is 30 seconds and so on.

1) Player finds a line on the court (baseline, sideline or free-throw line) and begins to jump over the line from left to right, jumping with both feet together, knees bent and hands above the head.

2) Repeat, but now jump forward and backward.

3) Repeat, but incorporate them together to form a box. Example: forward, left, backward and right.

4) Repeat, forming a W.

Minuteman/Lunge Series
1) Player finds a line on the court (baseline, sideline or free-throw line) and gets into a defensive stance. With the leg that is on the line, the player pushes off and lunges forward with the opposite leg, pointing the toe in the direction of the lunge.

2) Repeat, but increase to 2, 3 and 4 lunges consecutively.

3) Repeat, but turn and face the opposite way using the opposite leg to push off on.

Ladder Drill

1) Player sprints 1 full length of court in 5 seconds.

2) Three lengths in 15 seconds.

3) Five lengths in 30 seconds.

4) Seven lengths in 40-45 seconds

5) Nine lengths in 55-60 seconds

6) Eleven lengths in 65-70 seconds.

7) Thirteen lengths in 80-90 seconds.

8) Fifteen lengths in 95-105 seconds.

9) Repeat drill going down (15, 13, 11, 9, 7, 5, 3, and 1). Same times.

10) Allow equal time for sprint and then rest.

Coach Keith Holubesko
Five-Star Basketball Camp
Yonkers, New York

Rope Burn

Purpose:
Skipping rope is one of the most efficient ways to condition the body. This drill also emphasizes foot speed, body coordination and lower leg strength.

Organization:
We have our players do this workout three times a week. It is important that the rope moves continuously.

Time	Rate	Foot Position
60 seconds	moderate	together
30 seconds	fast	alternate feet
60 seconds	moderate	together
60 seconds	fast	together
20 seconds	moderate	left leg only
20 seconds	moderate	right leg only
20 seconds	fast	left leg only
20 seconds	fast	right leg only
20 seconds	fast	together
60 seconds	moderate	together

Total Time: 6:10

Bill Agronin, Associate Director of Athletics
Niagara University
Niagara University, New York

Tip-N-Sprint

Purpose:
To develop teamwork, ball control and cardiovascular endurance.

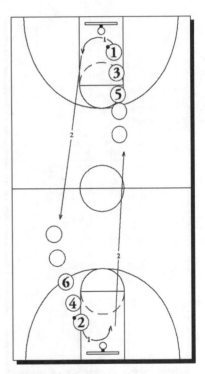

Organization:
Players divide into two units with one unit at each end of the court. Players 1 and 2 tip the ball against the backboard simultaneously and sprint to the opposite end. Player 3 follows and mimics 1; 4 follows and copies player 2. Play is continuous and lasts for a predetermined amount of time.

Coaching Points:
♦ Players must jump up and meet the ball.

♦ Players must not let the ball touch the floor.

Variations:
♦ If the task at hand is too difficult to youngsters, have them jump up, catch the ball, come down with it, then jump back up and shoot or toss it against the backboard.

♦ When a ball touches the floor, the time is started over.

Kevin L. Allen
West Florence High School
Florence, South Carolina

3-2-3 Conditioning Drill

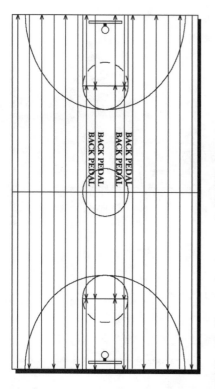

Contributor's Note: I wish I could take full credit for this drill, but I got this from Susan Walvius at South Carolina.

This is a great conditioning drill that employs sprinting, turning, and change of direction. In my practice I usually divide my team into post and guard groups. Each group will run the drill separately. Time is put on the clock.

This can vary, but I use 3:00 minutes as did USC. Players will first run three down-and-back sprints, hence the first "3." After the completion of the sprints, they will run from baseline to free-throw line. Once the reach the free-throw line, they will turn and backpedal until they reach the other free- throw line where they will turn and sprint to the end line. After reaching the end line, they will sprint forward to the free-throw line, turn and backpedal until they reach the other free-throw line, then sprint forward. This continues two times, hence the "2". They will then run three down-and-back sprints for the final "3". This is a continuous running drill. They have 3 minutes to complete the drill.

Coach Kathy Warner Corbett
Oglethorpe University
Atlanta, Georgia

Conditioning Full-Court Drills

Purpose: To warmup the team and improve overall conditioning.

Organization:

1) *Full-Court Lay-Ups*: Must make 90 lay-ups in two minutes. Players shoot first with right hand, then left hand. Coaches count made lay-ups (see diagram 1).

2) *Three Line Shooting*: Three players pass to halfcourt. Middle person takes a lay-up. Outside people get a pass from the baseline for a jump shot. Three people on the baseline go for a continuous drill (see diagram 2).

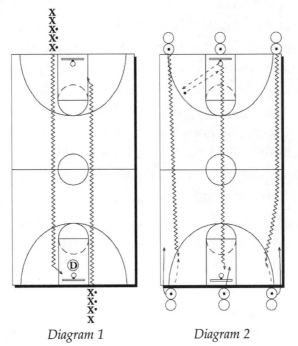

Diagram 1   Diagram 2

Coach Eric Stratman
Quincy Senior High School
Quincy, Illinois

Group Exercises & Conditioning

Purpose:
To get the team warmed up and ready to go at the beginning of every practice.

Organization:
1) *Fingertip Pushups:* Squad starts flat on floor; on whistle, they push up on fingertips until next whistle (usually 10 seconds). They then do 10 or more of these at their own pace, and this is followed by 10 more normal pushups using the palms of the hands.

2) *Arch Lifts:* Squad stands flat-footed; on whistle, each player springs from bent knees as high as she can and lands on her toes. Immediately, with arms fully extended above her head, she then jumps as high as she can without bending her knees (only from and onto her toes) 20 times. This whole process is repeated four more times.

   Then each girl, starting flat-footed, bounces up and down on her toes 20 times. She does a series of five of these.

   A stretching, even a painful sensation, will be felt in the gastroenemius muscles and in the achilles tendons when this drill is done correctly and completely.

3) *Ankle Walk:* Squad, in single file, walks the baseline on the outside of their ankles, turns at the sideline and walks on the insides of their ankles, turns at the 10-second line and walks on tip toes across the 10-second lines and turns and comes down the other sideline on their heels. Emphasis is on the stretching and working of muscles, tendons and ligaments of the ankle joint.

4) *Backboard Tipping:* Squad lines up in a single-file line. Lead player puts a ball up against the board. The next player steps forward, leaps and catches the ball with arms extended and, at the top of her jump, rebounds the ball back up against the board using only her fingers and wrists (see diagram 1).

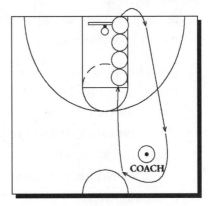

Diagram 1

Next woman gets the rebound and repeats. After tipping, a player runs around the coach and back to the end of the line.

A goal is set (100, etc.) before the drill is started and the drill continues until that many in a row are tipped correctly and the last one is made.

By stepping one step backward after each tip, the coach can require more running between tips and less standing around.

Variations:

♦ Have another ball going at the same time at the basket at the other end. A player must run to the other end after her turn at one end.

♦ Have two lines going at once at one basket.

♦ Have each player tip three or four times straight when it is her turn.

♦ After tipping, the player crosses the lane and the ball is tipped by the next player across the rim to her. She tips the ball back across the rim to the next player and then goes to the end of the line.

5) *Run-Shuffle Drill:* Players (spaced) run hard from court corner to free throw line extended. Each plants her outside foot and makes an abrupt change to a defensive shuffle step across floor.

At the sideline, players plant the outside foot and make an abrupt change to hard run to the 10-second line and then shuffle across the floor to the sideline. Players run forward to free-throw line extended, shuffle across, forward to baseline, and shuffle across end. This is one trip, and the squad continues until five complete, perfect trips are made by all (see diagram 2).

6) *Rope Jumping:* Often, half of our squad is jumping rope while the other half is doing the next drill (the block drill). They take about the same amount of time and the two groups can thus trade off equipment when they finish.

♦ For one minute: jump with both feet.

♦ For one minute: jump with right foot only.

♦ For one minute: jump with left foot only.

♦ For one minute: jump by alternating feet.

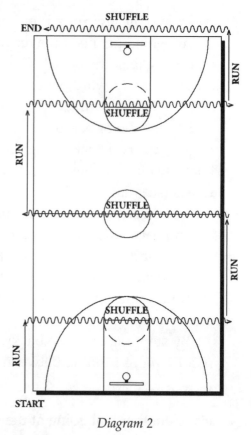

Diagram 2

Variations:

♦ Jump 20 times each with both, right, left, alternate and then start the series again and continue until the four minutes are up.

♦ Add tricks, such as:
  - double jumps (rope passes under feet twice in one jump)
  - crossed arms
  - backward jumping
  - boxer shuffle
  - rope folded in half
  - rope folded in quarters

7) *Block Drill:* Each player has three blocks. Blocks are made of wood and measure 2 x 3 x 4. Half the squad lines up down the middle of the lane. One block is in each player's hand, one is just outside the right lane line and the third is outside the left lane line. On the coach's whistle, the players all slide to the left with a good defen-

sive slide and head up and exchange blocks with one on the floor. They then slide back to the right, then the left, then the right, etc. Players go hard for one minute, then rest for 15 seconds. Repeat twice.

Variations:

- Two sets of 90 seconds.
- Three sets of 30 seconds *done twice as fast as normal.*

8) *Stairs:* Self-explanatory. Players must be watched to make sure each step is struck and that only the front part (the ball) of the foot is used.

9) *Barrier Jumping:* A subsitute for the old standard bench jumping. Barriers are made of electrical conduit (it bends) set in 20″ long 2 x 4 bases. (As an alternative, jump ropes held by two players and jumped by a third can work as well)

Complete two sets of 18 jumps the first night and increase by one each practice until players are doing two sets of 36. There is to be no little jump between jumps as there often is in rope jumping, it's jump-jump-jump-jump-jump, etc.

10) *Apache Drill:* One-half of squad lines up along the baseline. On the whistle, players sprint full speed to the free-throw line extended and change direction then run backward to the baseline and change again. They run forward to the 10-second line, backward to the baseline, forward to far free-throw line extended, backward back to the baseline, forward to the opposite end line, backward to the baseline.

Then they work their way back the same way, hitting the free-throw line, the 10-second line and, finally, the near free-throw line again. At each line, every player must pat both hands on the floor beyond the line. Each player goes twice to complete the drill.

Variations:

- Use a clock and compete juniors vs. seniors, tall vs. short, etc. Winner gets out of running the drill the second time.
- Late-season variation: have squad send one player to the free-

throw line. If she can make eight out of 10, the whole squad can skip this drill.

11) *Long Lay-Up Drill:* The players line up in two lines at the end line, facing downcourt. Each player in the left line has a ball. Each pair can use just three passes to go the full length of the court for a lay-up. There is no chance of not going full speed.

At the varsity level, drill will stop when no mistakes in passing, footwork or lay-up shooting occur during one complete squad trip. Lower levels adjust on number of passes allowed and acceptable percentage (see diagram 3).

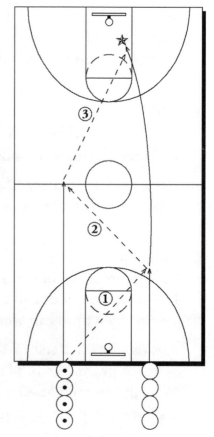

Diagram 3

12) *Super Rebounder Drill:* Player starts along the lane and throws the ball up gainst the backboard across the rim. She quickly crosses the lane and catches the ball. Her feet must both be outside the lane for the try to count. Players go for one minute or 25 "good ones," whichever comes first.

This is an excellent drill to emphasize that a good rebounder does not have to have the ball come to her side (see diagram 4).

Diagram 4

Coach Craig Kennedy
Auburn University
Auburn, Alabama

Crosscourt Conditioning

Purpose:
To improve overall conditioning, ballhandling skills and setting screens.

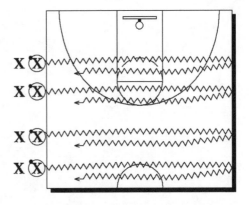

Organization:
This conditioning drill goes the width of the court. Make sure players touch the lines, stop and set good screens with hand signals and call their partner's name. Focus on execution when tired. Players can have water bottles at the end of their line to ensure that they stay hydrated if you wish. Always time this exercise to keep players putting forth maximum effort each time. Make sure everyone stays to encourage teammates to finish strong.

1) Put your team into groups of two or three on the sideline.

2) The first person in each line has a ball.

3) Dribble left-handed to the opposite sideline. Touch the sideline with a foot and return with the opposite hand. Do this three times.

4) Pass the ball when about five feet away and then set a screen for your partner.

5) Partner drives tight off the shoulder and dribbles left-handed to the other side.

6) Each group follows these repetitions. Three sets of "there and back" with the ball, pass and screen. One set of there and back, pass and screen. Three sets of there and back without a ball, tag off with your partner. Two sets of there and back without the ball, tag off with your partner. One set of there and back. On the last set, have athletes execute defensive footwork (slide) there and back, and then tag off.

Options include dribbling forward and backward, two-ball dribbling and increasing the number of repititions of defensive footwork.

Coach June Daugherty
University of Washington
Seattle, Washington

Team Toughness Series

Purpose:
The objective of these drills is to increase team toughness and conditioning.

Organization:
1. *Rip and Roll:* To begin the drill, have a coach or manager at the elbow with the ball. Players form a line from half court. Each player, one by one, passes the ball to the coach and then runs to the ball and rips the ball from the coach's hands. After the player has secured the ball, the player makes a power move to the basket and stays on the baseline.

   After the players go through "the rip" and end up on the baseline, the coaches then turn around to face them on the baseline. The player passes to the coach and the coach then rolls the ball out along the baseline. The player has to run out to the ball, pick it up, and make a power lay-up to the basket.

Coaches Notes:
Get players in the habit of calling the coach's name with each pass. Also, this drill is great with pads. Have coaches or managers stand in the key to hit the player as they make their move to the basket on rips and rolls. Since you can use both sides of the court, emphasize how crucial it is that they stay on their own side of the court to reduce the risks of players colliding with one another.

2. *90-Second 3's:* Players partner in two's. There are five different spots on the floor; players choose any five they wish. Player 1 has to hit three consecutive 3-pointers before they move on to the next spot. The goal is to see how many spots they can clear before 90 seconds expire.Coaches keep track of time and player 2 rebounds for player 1. After the drill is over, have each player call out how many spots they have cleared.

   This is also a rebounding drill. Player 2 should be going up hard for the rebound and making good outlet passes to player 1.

3) *Weave Shooting:* Players form three lines at half-court with the ball in the middle. Players do a 3-person weave and after the second pass, the shooter shoots. The other two players become rebounders and crash the boards. Do not allow the rebounders to camp out underneath the basket! If the shot is missed, the rebounder puts it back up, or she can pass it to the second rebounder if she has a better, closer shot. If the ball hits the ground, the score resets and those three players run to the end of the line. If the offensive rebounder misses the put-back, the score resets and the three players run to the end of the line. Managers keep track of points. 3's are worth three, 2's are worth two, and put-backs are worth one. Three minutes are put on the clock for this drill, and the goal varies. (After the ball hits the floor a few times, the players naturally get on each other. This is a great shooting, rebounding, and focus drill.)

4) *Skip "0" Shooting:* Players line up in three lines at half-court, with guards and wings on the outside lines and posts in the middle. The ball starts in one of the outside lines. The first pass can go to either the middle or skip to the opposite wing, and the wing can shoot the three. When the shot is taken, the other two players must crash the boards and put back the offensive rebound. If the ball hits the ground, the score is reset (the only exception is if the ball goes through the net on a score). Put three minutes on the clock for this drill and the goal varies.

Partner Drills

1) *Charge Drill:* Partners start on the baseline, opposite one another. X rolls the ball out towards the free- throw line. O runs out to get the ball and begins to dribble toward the basket. X steps up and takes the charge.

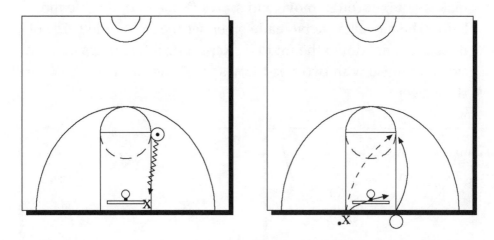

2) *Loose Ball Drill:* Partners start on baseline, opposite one another. X rolls the ball out toward the free-throw line. O dives on the floor for the loose ball. Once the ball is secured, O makes a pass to X from the ground and X makes the basket. Either repeat and switch, or alternate each time.

3) *Bounce Drill:* To begin the drill, X is positioned outside the key midway to the free-throw line. O or a coach bounces the ball hard so that it goes above the head of X. After the ball hits the floor on the initial bounce, X may react to the ball. X grabs the ball out of the air, simulating a rebound. X then squares up to the basket and makes a step-through move and scores (X may not dribble the ball). The move has to be made on either the right or left side of the basket, not down the middle. Repeat drill five times on each side and finish with two free-throws. If X misses a basket, the drill starts over.

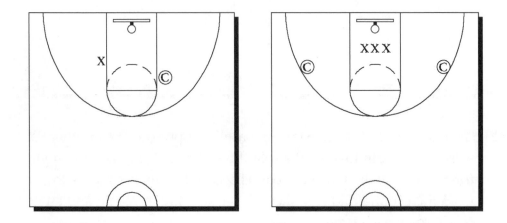

4) *3-0 Rebound Drill:* The drill begins with a coach or a manager on both sides of the basket outside of the key, and three players in the middle of the key. The coach throws the ball off of the backboard and the three players battle for the rebound and try to score without dribbling. The first player to three points wins. Emphasize boxing out after the shot on defense, and going hard to the offensive glass and following the shot on offense.

Husky Shooting Series

1) *Run the Line:* The drill begins with two people at each basket: a shooter at the elbow and one rebounder underneath the basket. The shooter begins at either elbow. She runs back and forth between each elbow for 30 seconds, and shoots at each one. After 30 seconds, the shooter switches to the wing and repeats the drill between the wing and the baseline. After the shooter completes this series, the two players switch positions (see diagram 1).

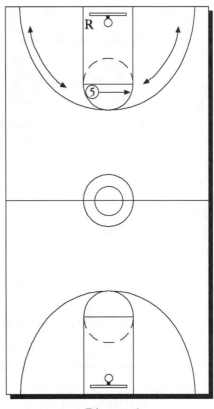

Diagram 1

2) *Beat the Clock:* This is a competitive shooting drill. The drill begins with two players at each basket: one is the shooter, shooting from seven spots on the floor, and one is the rebounder. Start the clock before the first shot is taken from the first spot on the floor. Each player must make eight shots from each spot (16 as a pair). When the first pair makes 16 shots, call it out and everyone moves to the next spot, with the shooters and rebounders rotating positions. The team that wins the spot by making 16 shots stays at the same basket, all others must move to a new basket for the next spot (see diagram 2).

Diagram 2

3) *Celtic Fastbreak:* Begin this drill with six players filling the positions shown in the diagram. Player 1 begins with the ball on the baseline

43

and makes a baseball pass to player 2, then replaces player 2 at the hash-mark line. Player 2 throws a chest pass to player 3 and fills the lane for a short jump shot off of a pass from player 3. Player 3 rebounds the shot and fills the line behind player 4 on the baseline. The same action is happening on both sides of the court (see diagram 3).

4) *Full Court "21" with Partner*: The drill begins with one shooter and one rebounder/passer. The shooter makes a lay-up and sprints out wide toward half-court. She receives a pass for a 3-pointer, 2-pointer or another lay-up at the other end. The rebounder sprints behind the shooter after she makes her pass

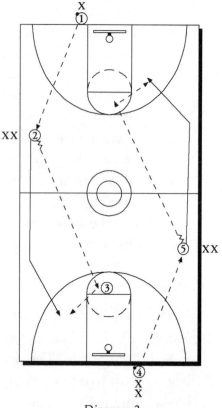

Diagram 3

because she will become the next shooter. The shooter rebounds her shot and passes to her partner for a lay-up. The drill continues until one player has scored 21 points.

CHAPTER TWO

Ballhandling & Game Conditioning Dribbling Drills

Duffy Burns, Former Coach
Cleveland State University
Cleveland, Ohio

The Daily Dozen

Diagram 1

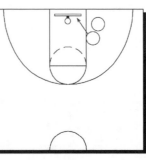

Diagram 2

Diagram 3

Purpose:
To improve game conditioning, ballhandling and shooting.

Diagram 4

Organization:
1) Underhand lay-up (See diagram 1):
   a) Dribble right
   b) Plant with left foot
   c) Shoot right

2) Overhand lay-up (See diagram 2):
   a) Dribble right
   b) Plant with left foot
   c) Shoot right

3) Under same hand (See diagram 3):
   a) Dribble right
   b) Plant with left foot
   c) Shoot right

Diagram 5

Diagram 6

Diagram 7

Diagram 8

Diagram 9

Diagram 10

Diagram 11

4) Under opposite hand (See diagram 4):
    a) Dribble right
    b) Plant with right foot
    c) Shoot left

5) Slide (See diagram 5):
    a) Dribble right
    b) Jump stop
    c) Shoot right or left

6) Roll hook (See diagram 6):
    a) Dribble left
    b) Plant with right foot
    c) Shoot left

7) Underhand lay-up (See diagram 7):
    a) Dribble left
    b) Plant with right foot
    c) Shoot left

8) Overhand lay-up (See diagram 8):
    a) Dribble left
    b) Plant with right foot
    c) Shoot left

9) Underhand same hand (See diagram 9):
    a) Dribble left
    b) Plant with right foot
    c) Shoot left

10) Under opposite hand (See diagram 10):
    a) Dribble left
    b) Plant with right foot
    c) Shoot right

11) Slide (See diagram 11):
    a) Dribble left
    b) Jump stop
    c) Shoot right or left

12) Roll hook (See diagram 12):
    a) Dribble right
    b) Plant with left foot
    c) Shoot right

Diagram 12

Coach Nelson Schorr
SUNY Potsdam
Potsdam, New York

Change-of-Direction Drill

Purpose:
To improve ballhandling, change of direction, individual moves and help-side defense.

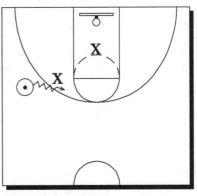

Diagram 1: Defender stops in the middle, reverses and changes direction.

Organization:

1) Offensive player starts out on the wing, one step out from the three-point line. Two defenders are playing defense. One of them is coming from the elbow and the other will come from the help side.

2) The offensive player takes one dribble toward the elbow defender who tries to stop her from going to the middle.

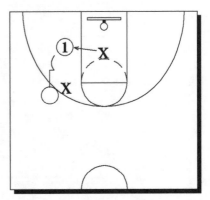

Diagram 2: Defender stops at the baseline. Offensive player changes direction and goes to the middle.

3) The offensive player then changes direction on the dribble and starts to go to the baseline.

4) The weakside defender comes from the lane and stops the offensive player from getting to the baseline.

5) The offensive player then changes direction on the dribble again and goes into the lane to shoot a short jump shot.

49

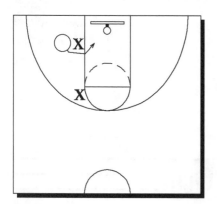

Diagram 3: Offensive player goes to the middle.

Coaching Points:
The offensive player uses three dribbles to accomplish the drill. The players would then rotate and go the other side of the floor and do the drill again.

Coach Kathy Warner Corbett
Oglethorpe University
Atlanta, Georgia

Dribble Drills

Purpose: To improve ballhandling.

Organization:

1) Dribble Tag

a) Each player starts with a basketball. They begin dribbling on the whistle and must continue dribbling while trying to knock balls away from the others.

b) If a player picks up the ball or double dribbles, she is out and must take the ball and sit on the sideline.

c) If a player steps out of bounds, she is out (set boundaries depending on your number of players — half of the court is usually effective).

d) As the game continues and more people get out, the boundaries will need to be made smaller.

e) Play continues until you have one winner.

2) Two-Ball Drag Dribble

a) With a ball in each hand, players walk slowly backward *dragging* balls in front of them. Keep the ball very low to the ground, use only fingertips and keep elbows completely straight. Players do this until they reach halfcourt.

b) Players walk forward from halfcourt, dragging the balls just behind each ankle very low to the ground (make sure they keep ball *behind* ankle).

3) Two-Ball Dribble Figure Eight

a) With one ball in the right and one ball in the left hand, drag the ball in left hand around left leg. Keep ball very low to the ground using only fingertips while continuing to dribble the ball in right hand off to the right side (very low to the ground). Continue the process with the other hand. Do not cross balls from right hand to left hand.

Coach Jack Miller
Rider University
Lawrenceville, New Jersey

Ballhandling Movement Drills

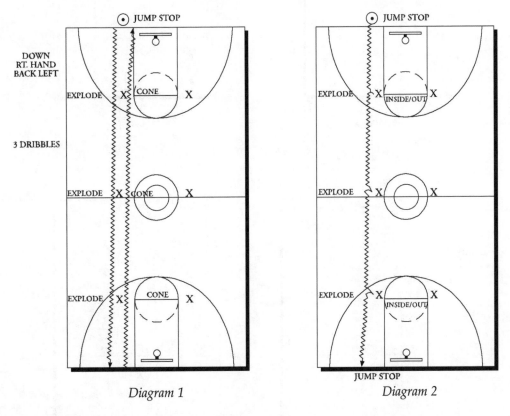

Diagram 1   Diagram 2

Purpose: To improve ballhandling skills

Organization:

1) Right hand controlled full court with three dribbles and explode by the defender or cone at free-throw line/halfcourt/free-throw line/ end line. Jump stop and switch to left hand and repeat (20 seconds total, 10 seconds down and 10 seconds back). See diagram 1.

FIVE-STAR GIRLS BASKETBALL DRILLS

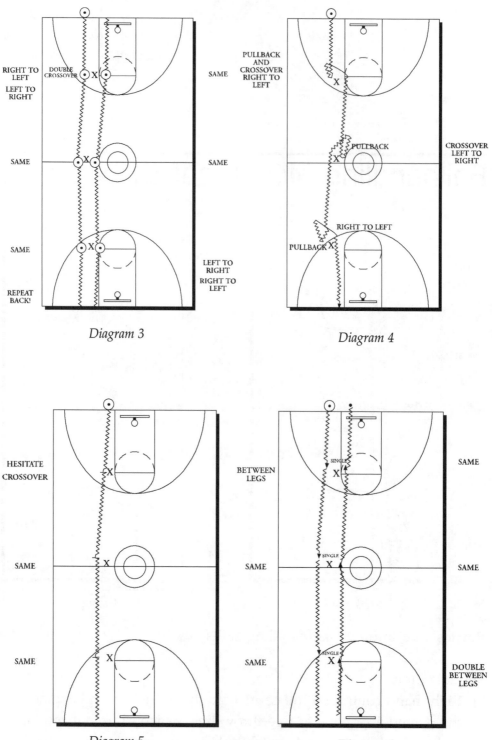

Diagram 3

Diagram 4

Diagram 5

Diagram 6

2) Right hand on side, perform a protected inside-out dribble on same side of body with same hand to free-throw line/halfcourt/free-throw line/end line. Then switch to left hand after jump stop and continue (20 seconds total, 10 seconds down and 10 seconds back). See diagram 2.

3) Dribble drive, double crossover fast and strong at all divisions on the court. Same coming back (20 seconds). See diagram 3.

4) Pullback, crossover move. Take two dribbles back out of trap and then explode into a crossover dribble (20 seconds total, 10 seconds down and 10 seconds back). See diagram 4.

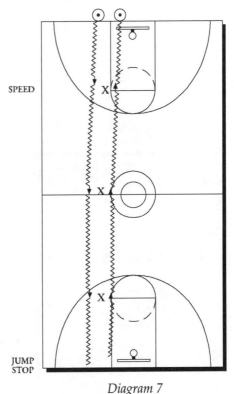

Diagram 7

5) Hesitation move, shuffle at defender/cone, then take a big step by while changing pace with crossover dribble (20 seconds total, 10 seconds down and 10 seconds back). See diagram 5.

6) Between the legs at each line. Single going down and double going back (20 seconds). See diagram 6.

7) Speed dribbling into jump stop, reverse pivot on end lines going down and back, right and left hand (20 seconds). See diagram 7.

8) Cooldown (40 seconds.)

Total Workout Time: 10 minutes

Coach Eric Stratman
Quincy Senior High School
Quincy, Illinois

Group Ballhandling Drills

Purpose:
To improve overall ballhandling and passing skills.

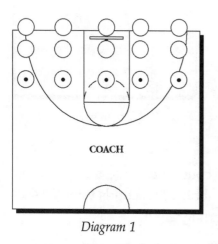

Diagram 1

Organization:

1) *Heads-Up Drill:* First player in each line has a ball. The coach signals movement of dribbling with hand. Players have to keep their head up and dribble at the same time (see diagram 1). This is an excellent drill with younger players and can be used for defensive slide work and conditioning also. Delays can be designed and used when players are executing the drill.

This drill also provides an excellent opportunity to practice pivot footwork. Front player can dribble out, stop, pivot and return to pass to the next player in line. All four pivots should be practiced: forward right, forward left, reverse right and reverse left.

2) *Peripheral Vision Drill:* Two balls are used. Player in middle keeps one ball going back and forth between herself and end player (see diagram 2).

The other ball is kept moving up and down between the middle player, the next player in line, the next, etc.

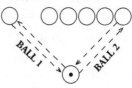

Diagram 2

3) *Bull-in-the-Ring:* Good drill for passing under pressure and, if you have a larger group of players, for practicing passing while being two-timed.

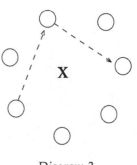

Player in ring must try to touch the ball as the other players pass it around. Passer can not pass to a player right next to her. If the player in the middle touches the ball, the player who is responsible for this is then put in the center

Diagram 3

(see diagram 3). With a very large group, put two or three players in the ring at one time.

4) *Pass-to-the-Outside-Hand Drill:* Players work in groups of six. Two groups at one basket, if desired, or groups at a basket.

Offensive players O1, O2 and O3 move the ball around between them by overhead passes. The opposing team (shown as X1, X2 and X3 in diagram 4) is on semi-defense. Player O3 slides and X1 does not front her in this.

Diagram 4

All passes must be made to the outside, extended target hand every time. All catches must be performed with the leg on the defender's side, crossing over properly during the catch.

All six players count passes aloud, and when 25 good ones are achieved, the six players exchange position.

This drill is also a good time to show younger players how passing can be achieved even though both are "covered." The outside hand pass coupled with the crossover leg catch make offenses work!

5) *Passing-on-the-Move-Drill:* This drill is run in 75% of our practices and can be run to either the right or left. Right-handed lay-ups result as show in diagram 5.

Six players begin at passing spots 2, 3, 4, 7, 8 and 9 as shown. They are changed periodically throughout the drill. Player 1 passes

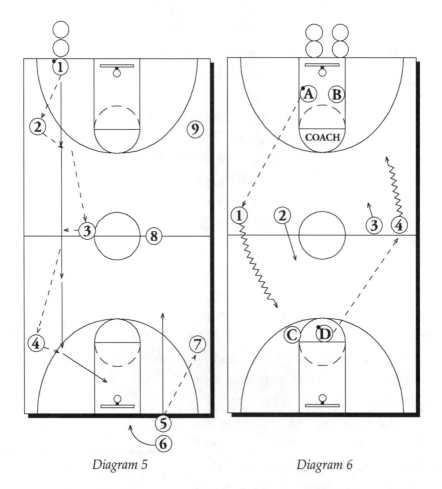

Diagram 5   *Diagram 6*

to player 2 and begins running straight down the court (at the same time 5 is passing to 7 to start the drill on the other side of the court). Player 2 passes to 1, who then passes to 3. Player 3 returns the pass to 1, who then passes to player 4. Player 4 returns the pass to 1 for a driving lay-up. Player 6 rebounds and passes to 7 to start down the other side. The same action is happening at both ends.

Variations:

♦ The game clock is set at the two-minute mark and the squad is required to make 25 lay-ups before the horn goes off.

♦ Sometimes do on only one side, rebound, give ball to permanent passer and then take off for long-pass lay-up.

6) *Diamond 2-on-2 drills:* Lots of emphasis on 2-on-2 play, checking out of shooter and outlet passing. Coach shoots and leaves floor. Teams A and B rebound and pass out to players 1 and 2. They attack at the

other end. Teams C and D defend against 1 and 2, rebound and outlet to players 3 and 4. They follow out to the 10-second line to be ready for next turn (see diagram 6).

6) *Ballhandling:* Squad lines up in two lines the length of the floor, about 12 feet apart. Players line up opposite a partner; one ball to a partnership. Each part of the drill is done eight times and the emphasis of this drill is on quickness.

 ♦ *Slams.* Ball is slammed from one hand to another.

 ♦ *Fingertip Flips.* Ball is flipped back and forth from hand to hand using the fingertips. Ball can also be moved above the head, eye level, waist level, knee level and back up through various levels.

 ♦ *Neck loops.* Around the neck, left to right then right to left.

 ♦ *Waist loops.*

 ♦ *Knee loops.* Around the right knee, then the left, then both.

 ♦ *Figure eight.*

 ♦ *Dribbling figure eight.*

 ♦ *Two-hand catches.* Ball between legs, body bent, both hands in front holding ball. Ball sent between legs (not touching the floor) and caught with both hands behind legs. Repeat and bring ball and both hands in front. Keep repeating.

 ♦ *Alternate catches.* Same as above only start with one hand in front of body and one behind. Keep switching while ball stays constant.

 ♦ *Chatter box.* Ball dribbled very low with alternate hands.

 ♦ *Tick-tock.* Ball dribbled one bounce through legs, left hand stays in front, right behind.

 ♦ *Clap catches.* Ball in front (or behind) at eye level and dropped. Hands clap behind and come back to catch ball.

 ♦ *Two-player catch.* Two balls and two players keep them going. Upon catching one, player whips between legs and out with pass to partner.

As more advanced drills are introduced, then the simpler drills at the top of the list are dropped.

Coach Dave Odom
University of South Carolina
Columbia, South Carolina

Stationary Ballhandling Drills

Purpose:
To improve overall ballhandling and passing skills.

Organization:

1) *Body Drill:* Controlling the ball with your fingertips, move the ball in circles as fast as you can.

   a) 20 times around the knees

   b) 20 time around the waist

   c) 20 times around the head

   d) Reverse directions and go back up

   e) Spread legs: 20 times around each leg

   f) Figure eight 20 times

   g) Cross-over dribble in front with right hand 20 times, then repeat to the left

2) *Dribbling Circles:* Ball as low to the ground as possible.

   a) Right hand only around right leg 20 times

   b) Left hand only around left leg 20 times

   c) Figure eight/reverse direction, 10 times in each direction

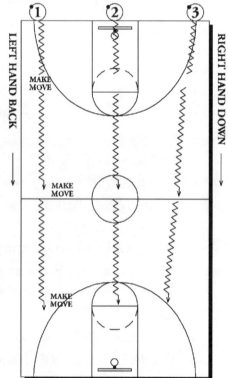

60

3) *Two Ball Drills:*
   a) Pound balls the same speed and height for 30 seconds
   b) Alternate balls 30 seconds
   c) Right high/left low 30 seconds
   d) Alternating balls dribble from baseline to baseline — then repeat using zig zag dribble

4) *Live Ball Moves from Baseline to Baseline:* Make move at each freethrow line and at halfcourt.
   a) Stutter step — try to get defender on his heels
   b) Crossover
   c) Inside-out move — emphasize keeping hand on top of the ball
   d) Pull back, crossover, pull

Coach Paul Culpo
University of Massachusetts
Amherst, Massachusetts

Full-Court Dribbling Drill

Purpose:

To practice change of pace and change of direction dribbling. To gain a better understanding of angles and footwork on dribble moves.

Key Concepts:

Great ball handlers have great footwork, understand angles and change speeds. You can take any dribble drill you like and use it every day in practice. If you do not teach these concepts your team's improvement will be marginal. Remember you want your players to dribble drive by the defense and be in a scoring position.

Footwork: Start each drill with the proper lead foot. Do you teach permanent pivot? Do you teach inside pivot? Be consistent. If you teach permanent pivot, then make sure that each player begins in that manner. If you teach inside pivot, then make sure to mix it up and have them practice using both feet.

When making a change of direction move, emphasize pushing off on the outside foot. In other words, if a player is dribbling to the right side and wants to change direction to the left, she would plant and push off her right foot, or outside foot. This is an important concept that must be mastered by effective ball handlers. Always push off on the oustide foot when making a change of direction dribble move.

Every move a ballplayer makes must be done on balance. Have your team practice keeping their balance. It may be a good idea to start these drills without a ball so that your players get the proper footwork down. Remember, a player off-balance is a non-player. Finally, emphasize that players need to be live dribblers. In other words, they must play on the balls of their feet — never on their heels. Get players to think of themselves as sprinters. A sprint starts by exploding off the balls of the feet. If a player is on the balls of her feet, she is ready to explode by the defense.

Change Speeds: I believe this to be the most under-utilized aspect in today's game. If a player has great speed and only plays at that top gear, she is only playing at 70% of her effectiveness. If a coach takes a player with above-average speed that plays at different gears, she will be the more effective player.

Angles: Attack! Attack! Attack! This is the mentality you want to impart through these drills. Players need to always go at the defender and make her move. Once the defender is on her heels, the attacker must take a very sharp angle to power past the defender "body to body." The diagram below illustrates this concept: If you are in a defensive stance and you slide laterally, you move effectively. Now, if you get in a defensive stance and slide backward... what happens? You have to turn your hips and drop step. It is a much slower process. So, do not allow the defender to get back in play. Tight angles are the key! Angles can make up for pure quickness. However, pure quickness cannot make up for bad angles.

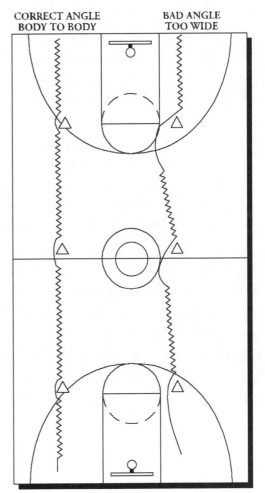

CORRECT ANGLE
BODY TO BODY

BAD ANGLE
TOO WIDE

Organization:

The drill runs baseline to baseline. Find cones or chairs, an any object that you can utilize on the floor at the spots marked "x" on the diagram. Break up your team into five groups of three. Put a group at each spot on the baseline. Have each group go down and back utilizing the specific dribble move at each object. Be consistent. Each player goes twice and then rotates to the next line. These drills are to be done at game speed. As the players become more comfortable, begin to introduce other dribble moves to substitute the ones below.

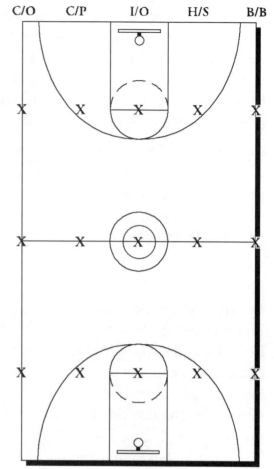

1) *Crossover Dribble:* Emphasize the dribble staying below the knees at the crossover and going at the defender/object and by it (shoulder to shoulder), rather than around it.

2) *Change of Pace Dribble:* This is the most overlooked weapon in today's game. Learning to play the game at different speeds can be a great offensive advantage. Emphasize exploding out of a half-speed dribble to full throttle at the defender/object (shoulder to shoulder). Ball should never get above the thigh area.

3) *Inside Out Dribble:* Players move by the defender/object by moving the ball to the inside of the body and then to the outside. Again, make sure that the players understand that the move is to attack the defender (shoulder to shoulder) and not to go around the defender.

4) *Hard Stutter Dribble:* Players must knock the defensive player back on her heels with a hard stutter and then accelerate past shoulder to shoulder.

5) *Behind the Back Dribble:* The key to this drill is that players must change direction only slightly. While we do not want to be in a straight line, we want to go at the defender and by her shoulder to shoulder. If the defender attacks the dribbler by reaching in for the dribble, then the dribble must utilize the change of direction from "first base" to "third base" movement. Otherwise, the dribbler must keep the angle tight and go by and not around the defender.

As a follow-up to these stations, remove all the cones/chairs and have each group return to their original spot. Put two balls with each group.

6) *Two Ball Dribble:* Emphasize the weak hand getting as good as the strong hand. Have the players go straight ahead and then zig-zag up and down the floor going the same way. Start everyone going to her left and then coming back to her right.
   ♦ Down and back simultaneous dribble
   ♦ Down and back alternate dribble
   ♦ Zig-zag down and back simultaneous
   ♦ Zig-zag down and back alternate dribble.
   ♦ Retreat dribble simultaneous
   ♦ Retreat dribble alternate.

On the reteat dribble, have the ballhandler take three hard dribbles forward and then retreat two dribbles. Simulate dribbling away from potential traps. This is a great drill and should be used as the climax of the workout. The ability to explode ahead and retreat with the two-ball dribble will pay great dividends in game situations.

Coaching Point:
Players must stay low to the ground and keep the head erect at all times.

CHAPTER THREE

Game Condition Passing & Catching Drills

Bill Agronin, Associate Director of Athletics
Niagara University
Niagara University, New York

20-Pass Lay-Up Drill

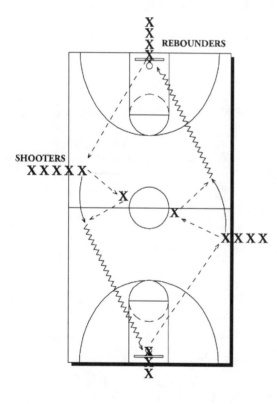

Purpose:
To work on passing, conditioning and concentration (making the lay-up).

Organization:
You will need a minimum of 10 players to complete this drill (12 to 14 works better). Place at least two rebounders at each end and two shooters at the hash marks. Also put a passer on each side of the half-court circle. The rebounder takes the ball out of the net and makes a good outlet pass to the shooter who is at the hash mark. The shooter passes to the passer at the half-court circle who then returns the ball back to the shooter for a lay-up.

Coaching Points:
♦ Stress good, crisp passes.
♦ Players must run hard.
♦ It will take a minute to get 20 or 21 baskets.

Coach Craig Kennedy
Auburn University
Auburn, Alabama

Four-Square Passing Drill

Purpose:
To develop passing and catching skils while utilizing a dribble screen.

Organization:
1) This drill requires four balls and eight or more people. Have the players form a square about 15 feet apart. Player 1 starts with the ball and takes a dribble or two and passes to player 2 (diagram 1).

2) Player 1 sets a screen for player 2 who dribbles around the screen then passes to player 3 (diagram 2).

3) Player 2 screens for player 3 who dribbles and passes to player 4. The rotation is dribble, pass, screen and replace. Keep going for one or two repetitions or until the players are comfortable. Have the players call out the name of the person they are passing to (diagram 3).

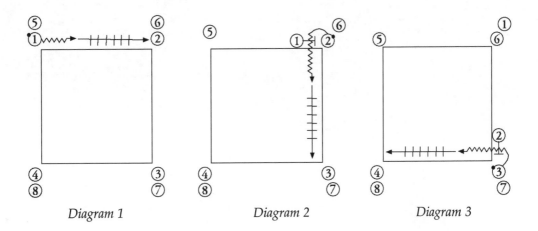

Diagram 1   Diagram 2   Diagram 3

4) Add a second ball opposite the first. You can add up to four balls. Change directions, go both clockwise and counterclockwise (diagram 4).

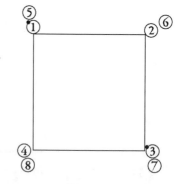

Diagram 4

Coaching Points:

♦ Work on hard dribble and getting close to the screener.

♦ Working on catching the pass off a screen.

Coach Cindy Griffin
St. Joseph's University
Philadelphia, Pennsylvania

Four Passes Drill

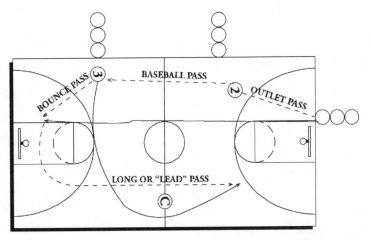

Purpose: To improve team conditioning, passing and communicating.

Organization:

Time = four minutes   Goal = 82 makes

1) Player 1 outlets to player 2.

2) Player 2 turns outside and throws a baseball pass to player 3.

3) Player 3 throws a bounce pass to player 1 who runs the lane line.

4) Player 3 runs outside "coach" and receives a long pass from player 1.

5) Player 1 sprints for a lay-up and sprints to touch the baseline after she passes to player 3.

6) Lines move in direction of pass or "follow your pass."

Cheryl Reeve, Assistant Coach
WBNA Charlotte Sting
Charlotte, North Carolina

6-Spot Passing Drill

Purpose:

This drill emphasizes passing at a quick pace with accuracy and finishing lay-ups by going up strong to the basket. Points of emphasis in the drill include passing, communication, finishing at the basket and conditioning.

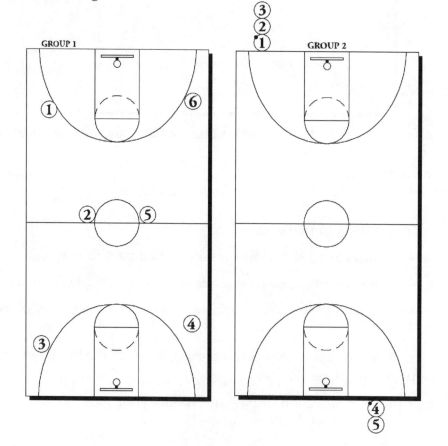

Organization:
Divide the team in half and put 2:00 on the clock. One half fills the six spots (group 1) and the other half (group 2) are passing and finishing lay-ups. Group 1 returns passes that Group 2 makes to them with the final spot on each side of the floor delivering a lead bounce pass that results in the lay-up. Group 2 splits in half with each group beginning the drill on opposite baselines. Players in group 2 should call the name of the player she is passing to and deliver a crisp chest pass to each spot while running hard in between the spots. At the final spot on that side of the floor, group 2 players will receive a bounce pass and finish the lay-up. Group 2 should do this for 1:00 and then switch with group 1. Group 2 would then fill the six spots and group 1 would pass and finish lay-ups.

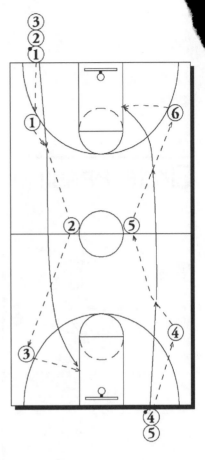

You could make this a competitive drill between teams with the team who makes the most lay-ups being the winner or you could give each team a set number of lay-ups they have to make in a certain time. These are good for keeping the pace of the drill at the desired intensity.

Coach Jill M. Pizzotti
Saint Louis University
St. Louis, Missouri

Circle Passing Drill

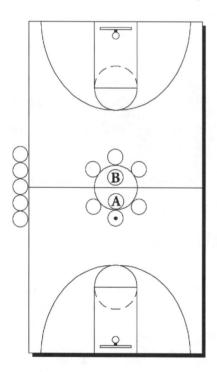

Purpose:
Teaches players pass fakes and handling pressure.

Organization:
Six players line up on the center circle. The remaining players are in a defensive stance along the side. (In the diagram, A and B are defensive players.) The coach gives the ball to a player on the circle. She must complete a pass to another player on the circle, but she cannot throw the ball to a player immediately to her left or right.

One defender guards the ball (A), the other reads where the pass is going. The defensive player stays in the circle until she gets a steal or deflection.

Bad passer or receiver goes to the end of the defensive stance line. The defender who gets a steal or deflection replaces the bad passer on the circle. The first person in the defensive stance line becomes the defender inside the circle.

Coaching Point:
We have the defensive stance line "chop" their feet as the ball is being passed in the circle.

Coach Craig Kennedy
Auburn University
Auburn, Alabama

Two Line Pass to a Lay-Up

Purpose:
To develop catching passes off the rebound and passing in transition.

Organization:

1) Put an outlet line on the side and a rebound line on the edge of the key. This drill requires two balls and at least eight players. The first person from each group steps onto the court. The coach or manager starts with the ball and tosses it off the backboard to simulate a rebound.

2) The rebounder makes an outlet pass to a side outlet (diagram 2). The outlet person can cut middle and call "middle" (diagram 3).

3) Player 1 cuts to the outside of the outlet person. Player A cuts outisde their outlet person. The outlet person dribbles upcourt (diagram 4).

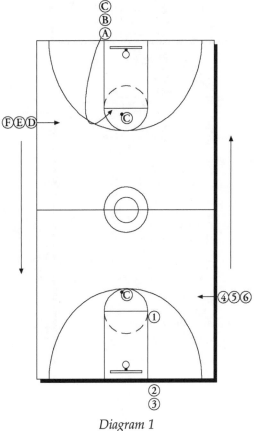

Diagram 1

75

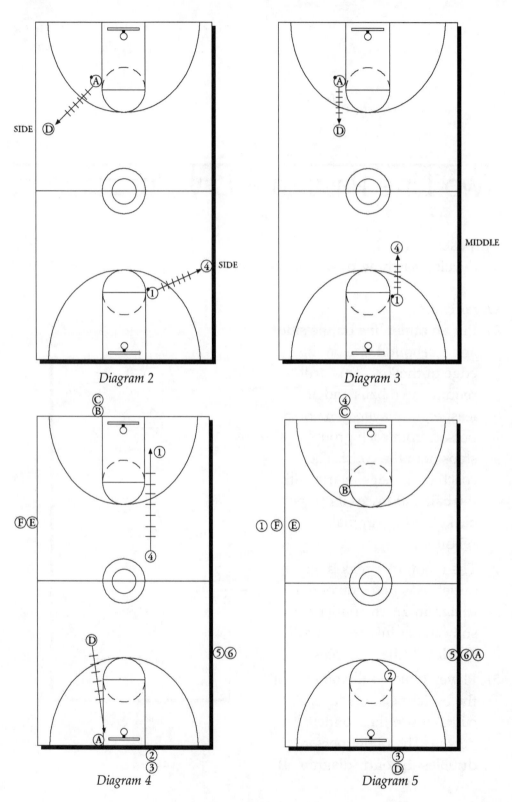

Diagram 2

Diagram 3

Diagram 4

Diagram 5

4) Player 4 leads the pass to player 1. D leads the pass to player A. The person doing a lay-up should be able to catch and go up without a dribble (diagram 5).

5) Players switch lines. The rebounder takes the ball and makes the outlet pass. Players switch lines when done one trip down the floor.

Coaching Points:

♦ This is a fast-paced drill that is also good for conditioning.

♦ Set goals for how many baskets are to be made in a set time limit.

Coach Craig Kennedy
Auburn University
Auburn, Alabama

Three Line Four Pass to a Lay-Up

Purpose:

To develop passing and catching in transition.

Organization:

1) This is an alternative to a three-player weave. To perform this drill, you need one ball and at least three players. Place three players in the key (see diagram 1).

2) The coach has the ball and tosses it up for a rebound or scores a lay-up (diagram 2).

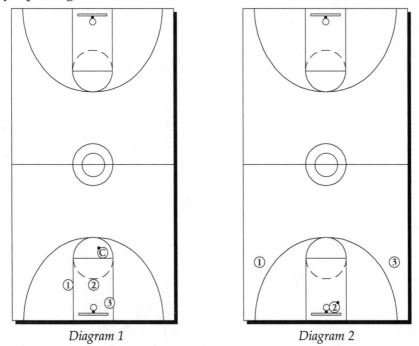

Diagram 1   Diagram 2

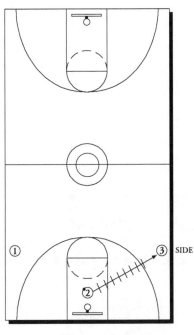

Diagram 3

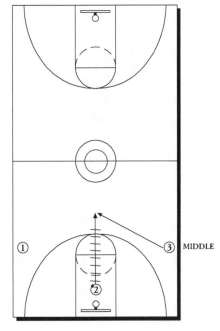

Diagram 4

3) In this case, player 2 has the rebound and players 1 and 3 have gone to the side outlet positions (diagram 3).

4) Player 2 passes to either side. In diagram 4, the person on the side calls "side." The drill can be run with the outlet person cutting middle (diagram 5) and calling "middle."

5) Player 3 takes the dribble down the middle of the floor. Players 1 and 2 fill the lanes (diagram 6).

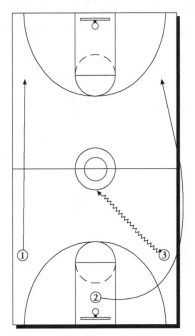

Diagram 5

6) As soon as player 3 is able, she makes a lead pass ahead to player 1. Player 3 moves into the point or pro position which is at the edge of the key extended (diagram 7).

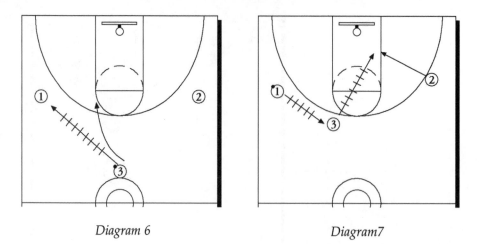

Diagram 6   Diagram7

7) Player 1 relays the ball back to player 3. Player 3 passes to 2 cutting to the hoop (diagram 7).

Variation:
To make this into a three line, three pass drill, eliminate the relay pass back to player 3. Player 1 hits 2 cutting to the hoop. Eliminating the relay pass means more hustle is required (see diagram 8).

Diagram 8

Coach Jessica Smith
Miami University of Ohio
Oxford, Ohio

Entry Passing

Purpose:
To work on a player's footwork while passing and to become more accurate on the pass.

Organization:
Players will need some masking tape or chalk to make an "X" on the wall or side of their garage at home. The player will take a ball and spin it out (toss it with backspin away from the target). As the player approaches the ball, she will square up and face the target, pivoting first on her right foot. She will make a bounce pass while stepping across the pivot foot (right). The player should continually visualize a defender that she must wrap the pass around. The player will aim for the target each time and check her accuracy. She must keep the ball low to the ground at all times and use her outside hand to make the pass. After mastering this passing technique, the player should practice passing while stepping away from her pivot foot. She must make sure to keep her pivot foot planted so she doesn't travel. Players must be sure to practice using both pivot feet.

Coach Kristy Curry
Purdue University
W. Lafayette, Indiana

Full Court Passing

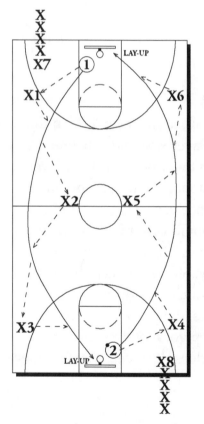

Purpose:

Improving passing, shooting, catching, communication and conditioning.

Organization:

Player O1 begins the drill by passing to X1, and runs down the court. O2 does the same with X4. O1 receives pass back from X1 and passes to X2 while continuing down the court. X1, after passing the ball back to O1 goes back to the spot where X2 is. X2 passes back to O1 and goes to the spot where X3 is. O1 receives pass from X2 and passes to X3. X3 receives pass from O1 and passes back to O1, who now shoots a lay-up. X3 follows O1 and re-bounds/gets the ball out of net and be-gins drill down the other side by passing to X8 who has taken X4's spot. O1 goes to the end of line behind X9. Both sides are going concurrently. Right Side: O2 to X4. X4 to O2. O2 to X5. X4 takes X5's spot. X5 to O2. O2 to X6. X5 takes X6's spot. X6 to O2. O2 shoots the lay-up. X6 rebounds and passes to X7.

Coaching Notes:

Kids request this drill daily going full speed passing, catching, com-municating and shooting. Be sure to set certain goals: no drop passes or push-ups, no missed shots or lay-ups, etc.

Coach Tom Shirley
Philadelphia University
Philadelphia, Pennsylvania

Outlet Drill

Purpose:
Improve overall team performance.

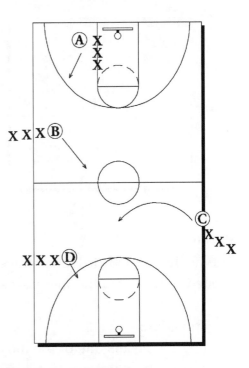

Organization:
Group A: Each player has a ball. Individually, they throw it off the glass and rebound. They throw an outlet pass to their partner in Group B.

Group B: Players catch the outlet pass and dribble once or twice toward the center circle.

Group C: Players move toward Group B players to receive pass and dribble hard once or twice toward the foul line and pass to shooter in Group D.

Group D: Each player shoots the ball as directed by the coach (off dribble, off catch, lay-up, etc.).

Reverse order to go back down the floor. Players are always moving, cutting, dribbling, passing and the coaches can step in and defend whenever.

Twelve-Second Drill

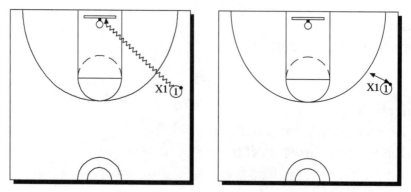

Diagram 1   *Diagram 2*

Purpose:

The twelve-second drill encourages patience and develops the skills needed to pass into the low post successfully.

Organization:

Feeding the post is one of the most frequent plays in basketball, but many players do not practice it enough and end up creating a turnover or giving up on the play.

Once a player receives the ball, she has a total of 15 seconds until she has to give it up. Five seconds on the catch, five seconds of dribbling and five more when she picks the ball up. The drill uses 4, 4 and 4 seconds to avoid close calls.

The drills starts with a player spinning out a pass to herself on the wing with a defender playing her. In the low post is an offensive player. After the catch, she must sweep the ball and step (pivot) to create space while looking to pass the ball into the post player. Once four seconds have elapsed, she must begin to dribble. The player must execute an up two, back two, pullback crossover dribble for four seconds while looking to pass inside. After four seconds, she must pick the ball up. She has four more seconds to sweep and step and pass the ball inside. The type of passes can be a wrap-around bounce, an over-the-head, or a lob. Be sure to fake a pass to make a pass.

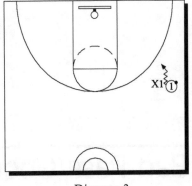

Diagram 3

This is a great drill that teaches a player to use her time efficiently, as well as working on passing in game situations. The results are less forced turnovers and more successful low post entries.

Coach Greg T. Collins
University of Louisville
Louisville, Kentucky

Bad Pass/Good Catch Drill

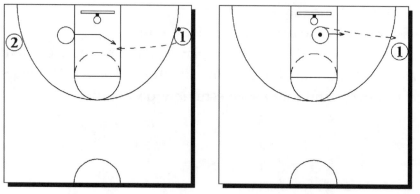

| Diagram 1 | Diagram 2 |

Purpose:
To improve a player's ability to catch all passes.

Organization:
One offensive post player, two passers on opposite sides of the court each with a basketball.

1) Player 1 throws a bad pass (too high, too low, etc.) and then calls the post player's name as soon as the pass is released (see diagram 1).

2) Upon hearing her name called, the post player turns and comes toward the bad pass, catches the pass and scores.

3) The shooter gets the ball out of the net and quickly passes back to the player who passed it. The post player simultaneously gets out of the lane (see diagram 2).

4) As soon as the post player's feet hit the floor outside the lane, the player on the opposite side throws a bad pass and calls the post player's name to continue the drill.

Coaching Points:
- Passers challenge the post player.

Coach Craig Kennedy
Auburn University
Auburn, Alabama

5-Spot Cut Drill to a Lay-Up

Purpose:
To develop catching and passing while utilizing the cut.

Organization:

1) This drill requires one ball and at least five players. Players line-up as indicated in diagram 1. Player 2 cuts away and back to the ball. Player 1 hits player 2 coming back hard to the ball. As player 2 is catching, 3 cuts away and then back to the ball. Player 2 hits 3 coming back to the ball. As the ball is in the air, player 4 cuts away and then back to the ball. Player 3 pivots and then hits 4. As the ball is in the air, player 5 v-cuts and goes back door and gets a pass from 4. Player 5 scores a lay-up (diagram 1).

2) Each player replaces the person they pass to (diagram 2).

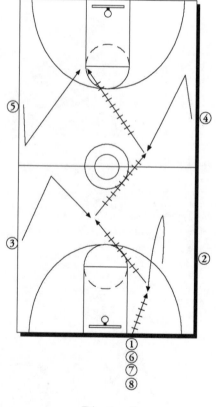

Diagram 1

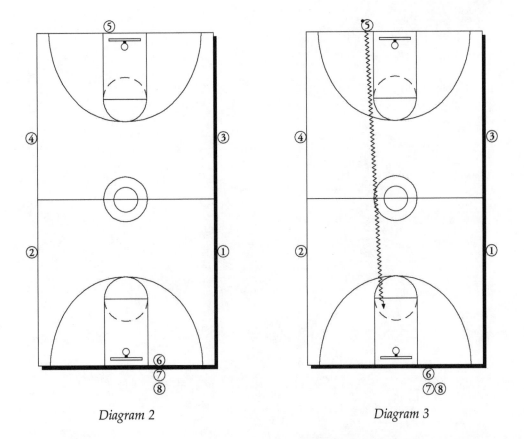

Diagram 2   Diagram 3

3) The person who scored the lay-up now goes the length of the floor and scores another lay-up. The next person in line grabs the ball and the drill begins again. The lay-up person goes to the back of the line (diagram 3).

CHAPTER FOUR
Shooting and Individual Offensive Concepts

Coach Brenda Frese
University of Maryland
College Park, Maryland

1:30 Free-Throw Drill

Diagram 1

Purpose:
To improve free-throw shooting.

Organization:
Pairup players and set the clock to 1 minute and 30 seconds. The first partner gets up and begins shooting her free throws. She must make three in a row to complete her part of the drill. Her partner rebounds the ball back to her (see diagram 1).

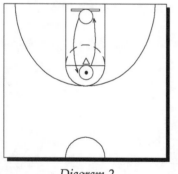
Diagram 2

Once the first partner finishes making three shots in a row, then the second partner gets up and shoots. She must make three free throws in a row as well. The second partner's time will depend upon the amount of time used by the first shooter. The two combined only get 1:30. If they don't complete the drill on time, we repeat the drill until they finish. This drill can also be done in a team setting, with one pair competing against another (see diagram 2).

Coach Sylvia Hatchell
University of North Carolina
Chapel Hill, North Carolina

3-Player/2-Ball Shooting Drill

Purpose:
To improve shooting and rebounding under game conditions.

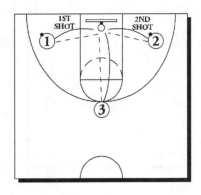

Organization:
Player 1 will shoot the ball, then go and get her own rebound and make a hard game-style pass to player 3. After player 1 shoots, player 2 will shoot the second ball and go get her own rebound and make a pass to player 1. Player 3 will shoot, then go get her own rebound and make a pass to player 2.

These three players will do the continuous shooting drill at a fast pace, taking game shots for a set period of time (usually one minute). Three new players step in and keep the drill going when the minute is up — rotation is shoot 3 minutes, rest 3 minutes.

Coach Cindy Griffin
St. Joseph's University
Philadelphia, Pennsylvania

30-Point Shooting Drill

Purpose: To develop three-dimensional shooting skills.

Organization:

1) As per the diagram, mark out five distinct spots for shooter to stand.

2) Each shooter will take three shots from a spot:

♦ First shot is a "3" — the player earns 3 points if it is made.

♦ Second shot is a shot fake and dribble to then pull-up hard and shoot — the player earns 2 points if it is made.

♦ Third shot is a shot fake and hard dribble to the basket for a lay-up — the player earns 1 point if made to the basket.

3) After the third shot from spot X1, the player moves to spot X2 and so on.

Partner rebounds and keeps score.

Coach Debbie Taneyhill
George Mason University
Fairfax, Virginia

Four-Minute Shooting Drill

Purpose:

This is a competitive drill we often use at the end of practice or right before a break. The team will shoot from each spot on the floor (both corners and both elbows) for one minute each. A coach is in charge of keeping score. A field goal is one point, a three-point shot is worth two points.

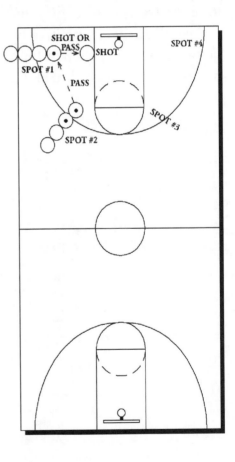

Organization:

Begin the drill with half the team in the corner and the other half at the elbow. The first two people at the elbow need a ball. The ball is passed from the elbow to the corner — shooter gets her own rebound and passer follows the pass and goes to the end of the line. After the shooter gets her rebound, she passes out to the elbow and goes to the end of the line.

After the first minute, both lines shift — the corner line goes to elbow, elbow goes to other elbow, balls stay in the same line. Shots now go up from the elbow.

Switch again after second minute — elbow to corner, elbow to elbow. Shots continue to go up from elbow.

To start the fourth minute, lines stay in the same spots, but pass comes from the elbow to the corner for shot. For the last spot, players have the option of calling "post" and running to block to receive the pass for a lay-up. (See the diagram, pass must go from elbow to corner to post.) Team must communicate.

Make the drill competitive by giving each team a target total of points. We try to get 80 or higher in four minutes. Total number of points can be adjusted to skill level and familiarity with the drill.

Coach Brenda Frese
University of Maryland
College Park, Maryland

Maryland Shooting Drills

Purpose:
To improve overall shooting ability.

Organization:

1. *5-Spot 3-Point Shooting Drill*: The object of the drill is to make a total of five three-point baskets from each spot. After making five from one spot, a player moves to the next spot. Drill can be timed to make it more competitive. Players can compete against each other or aim for a time under 2.5 minutes. (See Diagram 1)

2. *3 Players/2 Balls*: We then put three players on the floor with two balls to use between them. The first player steps up to the first spot as the shooter. We then set up one passer and one rebounder. The passer constantly feeds the shooter with balls, the rebounder rebounds and feeds the passer with balls. They do this until the shooter makes five shots from that spot (see diagram 2). After making five shots, the shooter moves to the next spot. The passer and rebounder move accordingly. They repeat the same action until the shooter makes five shots again. They continue this through all five spots. Once the drill is finished, the shooter will have made 25 three-point shots. (See Diagram 3)

Diagram 1

Diagram 2

Diagram 3

Coach Kevin Chaney
Solono Community College
Fairfield, California

Three-Point/Chair Shooting

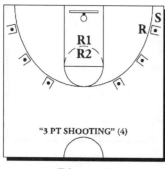

Diagram 1

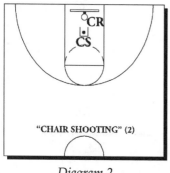

Diagram 2

Purpose:
To develop three-point shooting ability.

Organization:
At one basket, the shooter goes around twice shooting 11 three-pointers. The shooter is to focus on good and proper footwork and quick release (see diagram 1).

Footwork for three-pointers. Quick Release and hustling to each chair to simulate coming off screens to shoot.

At a second basket, place a chair just in front of the rim, start shot at 90 degrees and snap wrist up and out while shooting up and over the rim (see diagram 2).

This drill helps develop shot release, wrist snap and shot arch. Perfect for injured players too!

Rotation: S goes to CR position, R2 goes to R1, R goes to S, CS becomes R2, R1 becomes R, and CR becomes CS.

Coach Kevin Chaney
Solono Community College
Fairfield, California

"Circuit" Jump Shot Routine

Purpose:

To develop the jump shot. To break down the proper footwork to beat the defense and take a good percentage shot. Start at the #1 spot in diagram. Do the two-minute circuit, then move to spot #2 and repeat. It's a 10-minute drill, utilizing five spots on the court. The drill should always be done at game speed.

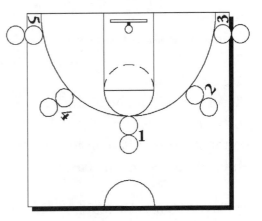

Organization:

Start by putting 10 minutes on the game clock. Assign two players per basket — more players may be added if necessary. Every player has a ball. Have players start at the top of the key. Blow whistle to indicate time to change position. The first 30 seconds are occupied by the players shooting the right, left, right jump shot. The next 30, flip pass right, left, right jump shot. Thirty seconds then are spent on the pump fake, step hop jump shot, and then reverse it for the next 30 seconds, pump fake crossover, step hop jump shot. Go to the right wing and repeat until all five spots are done.

Coach Jack Miller
Rider University
Lawrenceville, New Jersey

Competitive Shooting Drill

Purpose:
To improve shooting skills

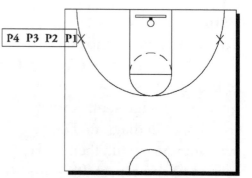

Organization:
Players start in a line at the left
corner of the baseline. Set a chair
on the three-point arc in the left
and right corner of the baseline.

1) Player 1 starts by making a one-on-one move around the chair. The
   progression of shots is as follows:
   a) Pump fake, swing the ball to the right, take one dribble to the
      middle for a shot.
   b) Pump fake, swing the ball to the left, take one dribble to the
      baseline for a shot.
   c) Pump fake, swing the ball to the right, take one dribble to the
      middle, then use a crossover dribble behind the chair, take
      another dribble to the baseline for a shot.
   d) Pump fake, swing the ball to the left, take one dribble to the
      baseline, then use a crossover dribble behind the chair, take an
      other dribble to the middle for a shot.

2) Players 2, 3 and 4 follow player 1. After each shot, the players go to
   the right corner and use the same shots. The progression on the
   right side is as follows:

a) Pump fake, swing the ball to the right, and take one dribble to the baseline for a shot.

b) Pump fake, swing the ball to the left, take one dribble to the middle for a shot.

c) Pump fake, swing the ball to the right, take one dribble to the baseline, then use a crossover dribble behind the chair, take another dribble to the middle for a shot.

d) Pump fake, swing the ball to the left, take one dribble to the middle, then use a crossover dribble behind the chair, take another dribble to the baseline for a shot.

3) First player to make 10 shots is the winner.

Bill Agronin, Associate Director of Athletics
Niagara University
Niagara University, New York

Continuous Lay-up Drill

Purpose:

To improve game conditioning and shooting.

Diagram 1

Organization:

1) A1 dribbles and makes basket, goes to end of B line. A2 follows up A1's shot and outlets to B1 (see diagram 1).

2) B1 passes to C1. C1 passes to A2, who sprints to the three-point line. C1 goes to the top line behind A3. A2 passes to B1 (see diagram 2).

Diagram 2

3) B1 passes back to A2 for shot (lay-up). B1 goes to end of C line (see diagram 3).

4) A2 makes lay-up, goes to end of B line. A3 shoots follow-up lay-up and outlets to B2. B2 passes to C2. A2 sprints to the three-point line (see diagram 4).

Diagram 3

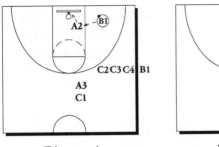

Diagram 4

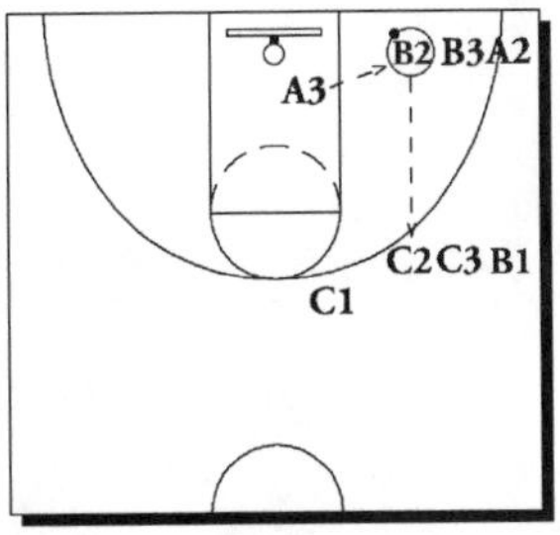

Diagram 5

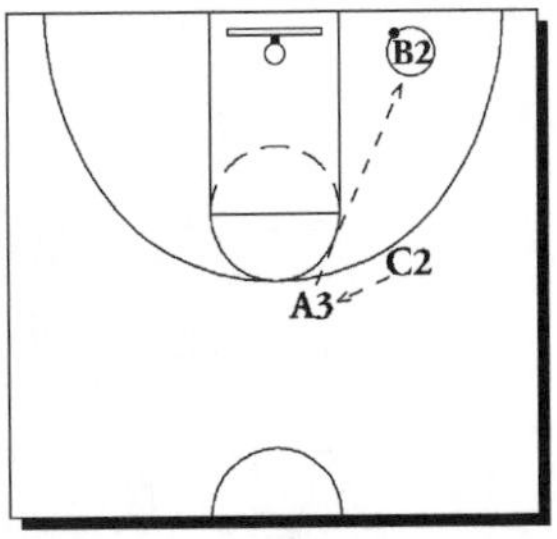

Diagram 6

5) C2 passes back to A3 then C2 goes to the top line behind C1 (see diagram 5).

6) A3 passes to B2, and A3 sprints to receive pass from B2. Drill continues until goal of made lay-ups is reached (see diagrams 6 and 7).

Diagram 7

Bob Foley, Former Coach
University of Richmond
Richmond, Virginia

Sprint Shooting

Purpose:
To shoot at game speed, game condition and game specificiations.

Organization:
All six passers (P) have basketballs. On the whistle, the S's run their fast-break lanes. The three P's pass to the player on their wing (or middle). The S's shoot, get their own rebound and fill the three P

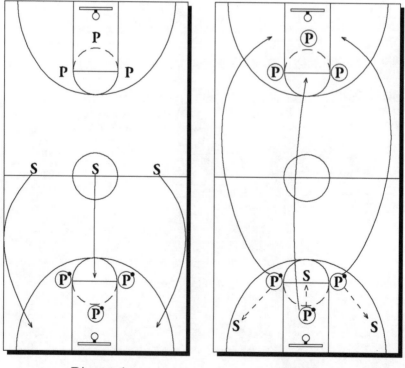

Diagram 1   Diagram 2

spots. The P's spring to their respective fast-break positions downcourt for a pass and shot.

We run this drill continuously for two minutes. We get great conditioning, shoot approximately 75 shots off transition, and the players enjoy it. We set a goal of 55 to 60 made shots and take a water break if successful.

Coaching Points:
♦ Run your lanes wide, full sprint into a controlled run, then into footwork for a balanced shot.
♦ We also make it mandatory that our wings shoot bank shots.

Coach Cheryl Dozier
University at Buffalo
Buffalo, New York

Star Shooting

Purpose:
To teach players to shoot properly when tired.

Organization:
This drill can be done with one or two
    players.

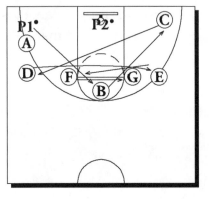

Diagram 1

1) Player 1 shoots first, while player 2
   rebounds and passes. Player 1 starts
   on the baseline and simply sprints
   from spot to spot catching and shooting.
2) After player 1 finishes her last shot (taken from the elbow), she
   follows her shot, puts it back if it is a miss, and then passes it out to
   player 2 for her shots.

Coaching Points:
   ♦ We emphasize the technical aspects of shooting: footwork,
     follow-through, body-balance, etc.
   ♦ It is also important that the player *sprints* from spot to spot to
     emphasize shooting while tired.

106

Bill Agronin, Associate Director of Athletics
Niagara University
Niagara University, New York

Three-Down Shooting

Purpose:

To improve three-point shooting. This drill can be used anytime during practice, but we have found it is most effective at the end as our last drill.

Organization:

You need a minimum of nine players to run the drill. There is no maximum, but, 12 is ideal. We begin with three players on each baseline and three players at half-court. Each player on the baseline has a ball. As the players from half-court run toward the baseline, a ball is passed to each player. After passing the ball, the passer runs toward the opposite basket. The players shoot when they receive the pass. A three-point shot counts three, inside the arc a jumper counts two, and anything in the "paint" counts one point. The drill goes for one minute. If the team scores a predetermined number of points, the drill is

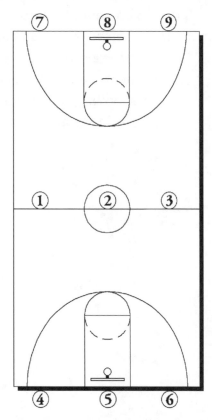

Diagram 1: *To start the Three Down Shooting Drill, put three players on each baseline and three at half court.*

over. If the score is not achieved, they do it again. We start the season with a goal of 60 points. As the season progresses we move our goal up to 65, then 70 points. Each shooter must get her rebound and be ready to pass to the next player coming down into her zone.

Coaching Points:

♦ A coach or manager should be stationed at each baseline to count the points.

♦ The players like the drill because it is competitive and there is a goal to meet.

♦ Coaches like it because it is a good conditioning, shooting and passing drill. You should emphasize squaring up before taking a shot and also making a good pass to the shooter. Limit the three-point shots to your better shooters. All others should shoot inside the arc.

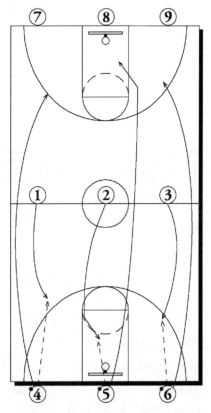

Diagram 2: *The passers move down the court to the opposite baseline ready to receive a pass and shot.*

Coach Sylvia Hatchell
University of North Carolina
Chapel Hill, North Carolina

Triangle Shooting Drill

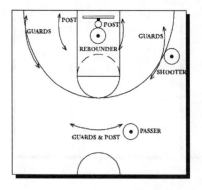

Purpose:
To improve perimeter shooting.

Organization:
The shooting area is three places on the court: right side, top and left side. Shooter will move within a 12-foot area. You have a shooter, a rebounder and a passer.

Rotate every 30 seconds (or 45 seconds or 60 seconds, depending on how long you have to conduct the drill). Use two balls. The shooter will shoot as many shots as possible in the time period allowed. Players will rotate from passer to shooter, shooter to rebounder, and rebounder to passer.

Coach Duffy Burns
Cleveland State University
Cleveland, Ohio

Daily Dozen II

Diagram 1

Diagram 2

Diagram 3

Diagram 4

Diagram 5

Purpose:
To improve game conditioning, ballhandling and shooting.

Organization:
1) *Lateral Cross* (diagram 1)
   a) Dribble right
   b) Jump stop
   c) Plant with right foot
   c) Shoot left

2) *Diagonal Cross* (diagram 2)
   a) Dribble right
   b) Jump stop
   c) Plant with right foot
   d) Shoot left

| *Diagram 6* | *Diagram 7* | *Diagram 8* |

3) *Step Around* (diagram 3)
   a) Dribble right
   b) Jump stop
   c) Plant with left foot
   d) Shoot jumper

4) *Glide* (diagram 4)
   a) Dribble left
   b) Jump stop
   c) Shoot right

5) *Runner* (diagram 5)
   a) Dribble left
   b) Plant with right foot
   c) Shoot jumper

6) *Jump Hook* (diagram 6)
   a) Dribble right — back player into block
   b) Plant with right foot
   c) Shoot left

7) *Lateral Cross* (diagram 7)
   a) Dribble left
   b) Jump stop
   c) Plant with left foot
   c) Shoot right

8) Diagonal Cross (See Diagram 8)
   a) Dribble left
   b) Jump stop

Diagram 9

Diagram 10

Diagram 11

c) Plant with left foot
d) Shoot right

9) *Step Through* (diagram 9)
   a) Dribble left
   b) Jump Stop
   c) Plant with right foot
   d) Shoot jumper

Diagram 12

10) *Glide* (diagram 10)
   a) Dribble right
   b) Jump stop
   c) Shoot left

11) *Runner* (diagram 11)
   a) Dribble right
   b) Plant with left foot
   c) Shoot jumper

12) *Jump Hook* (diagram 12)
   a) Dribble left — back player into block
   b) Plant with left foot
   c) Shoot right

Coach Charlene Curtis
Wake Forest University
Winston-Salem, North Carolina

1-on-1 Offensive Moves

Purpose: To develop a player's total offensive game and not limit them to one move. Basic 1-on-1 offensive moves when facing the basket can be used from any position on the floor.

Organization:
1) *Getting Open*: Use a change of pace with a change of direction to get open to receive the ball.
   a) V-cut. Turn your body toward the basket. Take two or three steps, plant your inside foot (the foot closest to the baseline), and push off toward the ball to receive the pass. Your movement is in the shape of a "V."
   b) L-cut. Start away from the ball. Take two or three steps straight toward the ball. Plant your inside foot and push off at a 45-degree angle to receive the pass. Your movement is in the shape of an "L."

2) *Receiving the Pass*: Call for the ball when you are ready to receive it. Extend your arms with your palms facing the ball. Your fingers should be relaxed and your elbows slightly bent.

3) *Facing the Basket*: Turning to face the basket allows you to see the basket, your defender and your teammates.
   a) Pivoting. Using your inside foot (the foot closest to the basket), lift your heel slightly off the floor, then turn and face the basket.

b) Triple-threat position. Position the ball in front of you so you can shoot it, pass it or dribble it. You may bring the ball to this position by swinging it quickly by your knees, across your chest, or up and across your forehead.

4) *Attacking the Defender*: All 1-on-1 moves begin with a short jab step made with the nonpivot foot (the foot farthest from the basket when you pivoted). The jab step may be a part of the pivot or an additional step after you pivot. The best offensive moves are made toward the defender's front foot. To simplify the explanation of these moves, the defender's front foot is on the same side as the jab step in all of these situations. Your left foot is your pivot foot and your right foot is your jab foot. (The same move can be made with your right foot as your pivot foot and your left foot as your jab foot.)

a) Jab step. With your knees bent and maintaining a triple-threat position, move your right foot forward while leaning slightly over the foot. This movement gives the defender the impression that you are moving in that direction. The jab step should be short enough for you to remain balanced.

It is important that you first work hard to get open; second, ask for the ball by calling for it and extending your arms, and then square up and face the basket. Attacking the defender's front foot makes the most effective 1-on-1 move. Take your time and read the defender's stance, then attack the front foot.

Coach Jessica Smith
Miami University of Ohio
Oxford, Ohio

Jab Series: Footwork

Purpose:
To master the footwork from a triple-threat position.

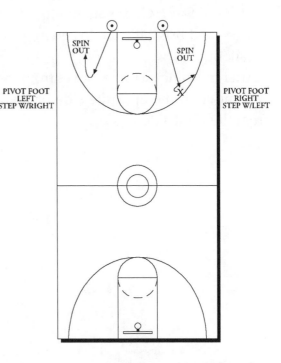

Organization:
The player begins on the left side of the basket about 15 feet out on the baseline. Before each move, the player will spin the ball out (toss it with backspin toward the free-throw line). As the player approaches the ball, she will square up to the basket on her inside foot (in this case, her left) as she catches the ball. She will bend her knees and sit down so she is quick in her motions. At this point, follow the individual moves for the players to work on:

1) *Jab and Go*: While squared up, the player will jab with her right foot (take a small hard step forward with only one foot, so she doesn't travel) and keep the ball on the right side of her body. Then the player will accelerate in that same direction by restepping with that same foot and taking a dribble on the outside of the right foot. At

this point, she explodes to the rim for a lay-up using one or two dribbles.

2) *Jab and Crossover*: While squared up, the player will jab with her right foot, with the ball on her right side, then swing the ball through to the left side with a quick sweeping motion at knee level and cross her right foot over her left (without moving the left). Finally, she will explode to the basket using one or two dribbles.

3) *Square and Shoot*: Once squared up, the player will go right into her shot.

4) *Jab and Shoot*: Once squared up, the player will jab with her right foot and bring it back to square position; staying low, she will then shoot.

After finishing all these moves from the left side of the basket, the player will move to the opposite side of the basket and repeat the jab series from the right side.

Duffy Burns, Former Coach
Cleveland State University
Cleveland, Ohio

Perimeter Moves

Diagram 1

Diagram 2

Diagram 3

Purpose:
To enhance the development of perimeter players.

Diagram 4

Organization:

1) Left foot is always the pivot foot. Direct cross (diagram 1).

2) Fake cross (diagram 2).

3) Back off (diagram 3).

4) Fake back off (diagram 4).

Coach Joe McKeown
George Washington University
Washington, D.C.

Snap, Crackle, Pop

Purpose:

To develop screening/base of the screen.

Organization:

1) Player X1 passes to the coach and screens for player X2.

2) Player X2 curls to the basket and X1 pops back for the shot.

3) Add defensive players and rotate.

Diagram 1

Diagram 2

Bob Foley, Former Coach
University of Richmond
Richmond, Virginia

Two Ball Screen Drill

Purpose:
Setting and using screens to improve footwork.

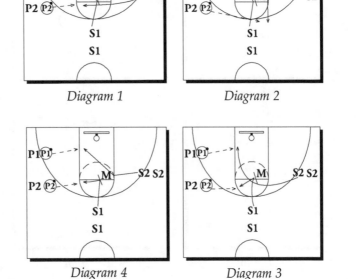

Diagram 1   Diagram 2

Diagram 4   Diagram 3

Organization:
Players start in four lines.
P = Passing Lines
S = Shooting Lines
S1 sets a screen on M (managers) for S-2.

S2 can (4 options):
  1) Flash to the ball
  2) Fade off the screen
  3) Curl to the basket
  4) Cut backdoor off the screen

S1 reads where S2 cuts and rolls to the appropriate spot. P1 passes to the cutter going to the basket, P2 passes to the cutter going to the high post area for a jumper. S1 and S2 get their own rebounds and get into the passing line. P1 and P2 go to the shooting lines.

The drill focuses on how to read screens and how the screener reacts to that read. We also stress the footwork on the approach and the explosion off the screens, as well as the screener coming back to the ball and looking for her own shot.

119

Duffy Burns, Former Coach
Cleveland State University
Cleveland, Ohio

12 Ways to 3

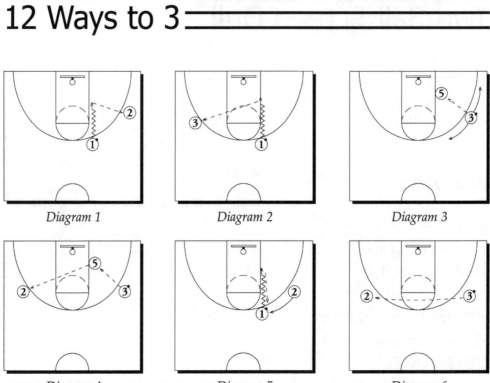

| Diagram 1 | Diagram 2 | Diagram 3 |

| Diagram 4 | Diagram 5 | Diagram 6 |

Purpose:

To break down every possible 3-point opportunity that a team might get in transition or on offense.

Organization:

1) Penetrate and pitch — same side (diagram 1).

2) Penetrate and pitch — opposite side (diagram 2).

3) Inside-out — same side (diagram 3).

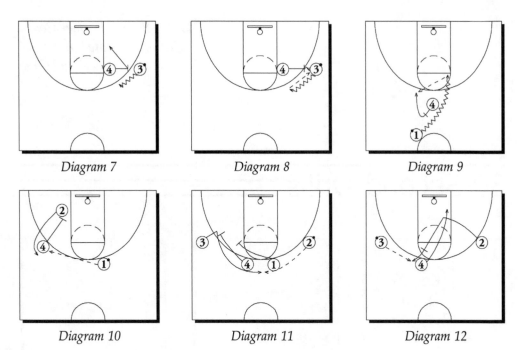

Diagram 7   Diagram 8   Diagram 9

Diagram 10   Diagram 11   Diagram 12

4) Inside-out — opposite side (diagram 4).

5) Fill the hole (diagram 5).

6) Skip pass (diagram 6).

7) Screen-and-roll (diagram 7).

8) Screen-and-pop (diagram 8).

9) Screen-and-pop — top of key (diagram 9).

10) Deep curl (diagram 10).

11) Staggered double (diagram 11).

12) Back-screen lob (diagram 12).

Duffy Burns, Former Coach
Cleveland State University
Cleveland, Ohio

30-Second Drills

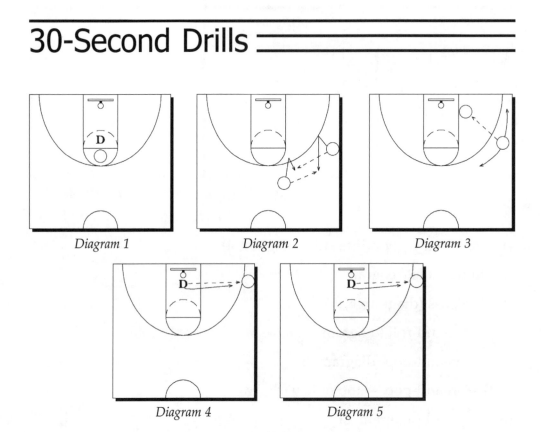

Diagram 1   *Diagram 2*   *Diagram 3*

Diagram 4   *Diagram 5*

Purpose:

To break down different aspects of offense and rebounding and enhance the "team" concept. Repetition creates good habits.

Organization:

1) *Pivot and protect* (diagram 1)

2) *Passing and cutting* (diagram 2)

3) *Pass and relocate* (diagram 3).

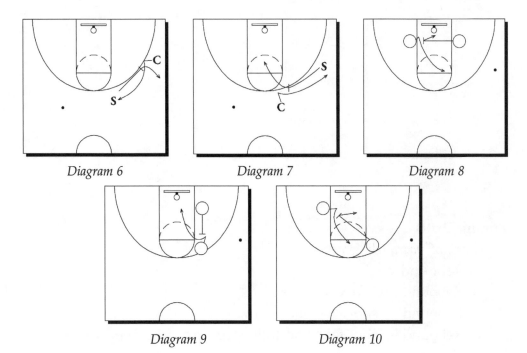

Diagram 6   Diagram 7   Diagram 8

Diagram 9   Diagram 10

4) *Run at the shooter*: (See Diagram 4)
   Paired shooting — 5 spots
      a) Shoulders in front of feet
      b) Hands ready
      c) Catch and shoot
      d) Make 5, rotate to next spot

   Paired shooting with shot fake and one dribble (diagram 5)
      a) Shot fake — shooting pocket to forehead
      b) One dribble — go thru defense

5) *Buddy screening* (perimeter) down screen (diagram 6)

6) *Back screen* (diagram 7)

7) *Buddy screening (inside) cross screen* (diagram 8)

8) *Back screen* (diagram 9)

9) *Down screen* (diagram 10)

FIVE-STAR GIRLS BASKETBALL DRILLS

Diagram 11   Diagram 12   Diagram 13

Timing Drills

1) *Throw off board* (diagram 11)
   a) Rebound
   b) Rebound and follow
   c) Rebound — shot fake and follow
   d) Rebound — shot fake and follow reverse lay-up
   e) Tip-in
   f) Rebound — back rim and follow (backboard)
   g) Tipping and touching (McHale Drill)

2) *Rebound and outlet* (diagram 12)
   a) Rebound — outlet
   b) Post up — move
   c) Bang the board (3 times)

3) *Post moves* (1-on-1 moves) (diagram 13)
   a) No dribble
   b) 1 dribble

4) *Perimeter moves*
   a) 1 dribble
   b) 2 dribble

Coach Belinda "Boe" Pearman
University of Rhode Island
Kingston, Rhode Island

Zone Coverage Breakdown

| Diagram 1 | Diagram 2 | Diagram 3 |

Purpose:
Work on zone coverage in breakdown situations.

Organization:
1) *Guard Coverage*: Set up the drill with two guards on defense and four offensive players outside the three-point line.
   a) Player starts with ball and defenders must guard ball and defend the next pass.
   b) Offensive players remain stationary and pass the ball only on coach's command.

2) *Post Coverage*
   a) Coach passes ball to the corner offensive player and wing defender must cover, while post defender goes "top side" to baseline coverage.
   b) On pass to high post, post defender goes "top side" and wing defender comes back to coverage.

Coach Craig Kennedy
Auburn University
Auburn, Alabama

Initiating a Drive

Purpose:
This drill teaches players to learn how to read the defender and drive for a lay-up or jump shot.

Organization:
Set goals of so many made hoops in a row, or a total number of shots. You need a minimum of three people and one basketball. The rotation is always as follows: follow your pass and play cooperative or live defense, replace the person you guard, score, rebound, pass, play defense and replace.

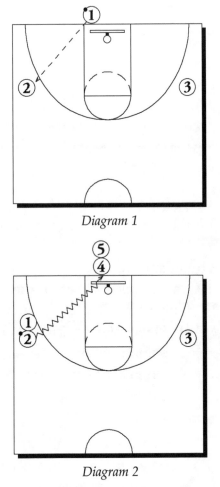

Diagram 1

Diagram 2

Have players in three lines under the basket with the ball in the middle line (diagram 1). Player 1 has the ball and passes out to 2. Player 1 goes and plays defense on 2. At first have the defenders play cooperative defense and take away a designated side, either baseline or middle. Drills can become operational or live after players learn to read and respond. The defender now replaces 2 on the wing (diagram 2). Player 2 drives around the defender for a lay-up (diagram 3). Player 2 finishes her shot if she misses, and then goes to

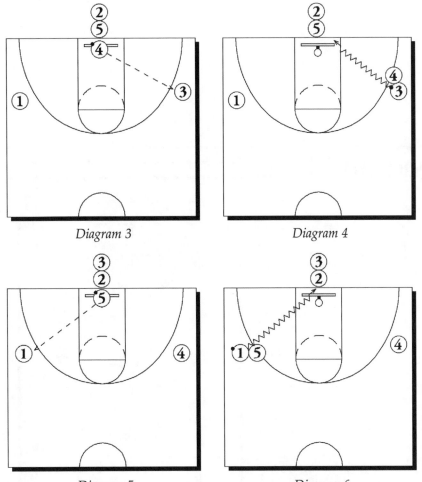

Diagram 3   Diagram 4

Diagram 5   Diagram 6

the back of the line. Player 4 passes out to 3, and plays defense (diagram 4). Player 3 drives at the defender for a lay-up (diagram 5). Player 3 finishes her shot if missed. Player 5 passes the ball and goes and plays defense on 1 (diagram 6).

This drill can be the same as "screen to three jumpers" and use only three players at each hoop. Players can learn to use shot fakes to bring the defender out to create space for the drive. Have players finish off if they miss, and always catch the rebound in the air. Encourage the last person to drive in for a lay-up or a close jumper if the first two have missed, so that players understand the need to take a high-percentage shot and stop their own scoring slumps. This drill also moves nicely into a 2-on-1 full-court drill or a 2-on-1 half-court drill if the coach wants.

Coach Craig Kennedy
Auburn University
Auburn, Alabama

Read and Lead

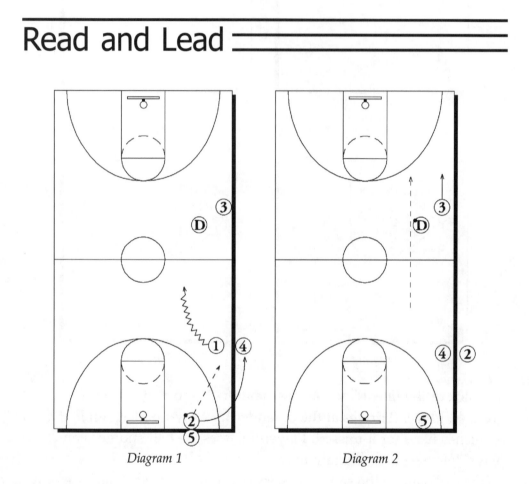

Diagram 1   Diagram 2

Purpose:

This drill teaches players to read the defender on a transition situation.

Organization:

Have one group of players on the end line to rebound and one group on the sideline at the outlet position. Have another group at the other end, but on the same side of the floor at the time line. Have a defender downcourt who can either look to deny the lead pass or protect the

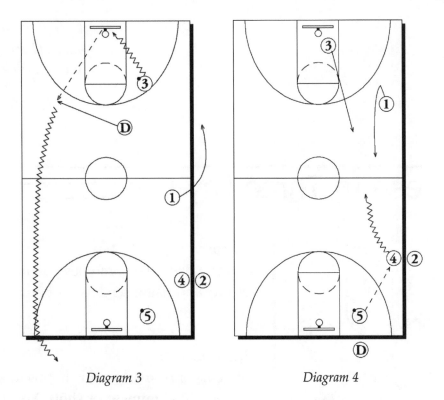

Diagram 3   *Diagram 4*

basket (diagram 1). Player 2 tosses the ball off of the backboard to simulate a rebound and then makes an outlet pass to player 1. Player 2 passes and goes to the back of the outlet line (diagram 1).

Player 1 takes the ball on the dribble and reads when her teammate 3 is open. Player 1 has to pass before she crosses the center line (diagram 2). When player 3 gets the ball, she goes one-on-one with D. After scoring, player 3 makes an outlet pass to the defender "D" who goes the length of the floor for a lay-up or jump shot and joins the rebound line.

The person who played offense during one-on-one (3) now becomes the defender, the person who made the lead pass (1) now becomes the offensive player for one-on-one. The next player in the outlet line steps onto the court. The rebounder tosses the ball up off of the backboard and the drill continues (diagram 4).

This is another drill that can become a 2-on-1 on the way back if the coach desires. Have the defenders vary whether they will deny or protect so that the ball handler learns to "read and respond" and make the appropriate pass.

Coach Craig Kennedy
Auburn University
Auburn, Alabama

Screen to Three Lay-ups

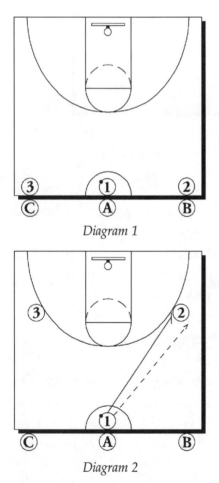

Diagram 1

Diagram 2

Purpose:
This is a drill that combines passing, setting, and using screens for both a shot or a drive.

Organization:
Set goals of so many made hoops in a row or a total number or shots. You need a minimum of three people and one basketball. The rotation is always as follows: follow your pass and set a ball screen, replace the person you screen, score, rebound, pass, ball screen and replace.

Have players in three lines at center with the ball in the middle line (diagram 1). Player 1 has the ball and passes ahead to 2. Player 1 sets a ball screen for 2 and replaces 2 on the wing (diagram 2). Player 2 drives around the screen for a lay-up (diagram 3). Player 2 finishes her shot if she misses, and rebounds her own shot. Player 2 passes out to 3 and sets a ball screen (diagram 4). Player 3 drives off of the screen for a lay-up (diagram 5). Player 3 rebounds her own shot and passes and ball screens for 1 (diagram 6).

Player 1 drives for a lay-up and rebounds her own shot (diagram 7). To complete the drill, player 1 makes an outlet pass and the outlet

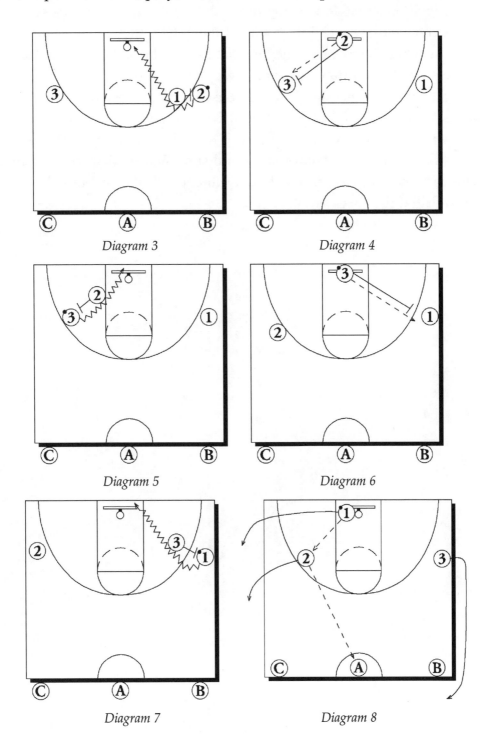

Diagram 3

Diagram 4

Diagram 5

Diagram 6

Diagram 7

Diagram 8

relays the ball to the middle person of the next group (diagram 8). 1-2-3 go off the side of the court so that next group can go.

This drill can be done using jump shots around or over the screen. I like to have players call the name of the person they are screening for and use a hand signal to indicate what side of the screen to use. Have players finish off if they miss and always catch the rebound in the air. When shooting jump shots, I have consequences when all three do not score. Encourage the last person to drive in for a lay-up or a close jumper if the first two have missed so that players understand the need to take high percentage shots and stop their own scoring slumps. This drill moves nicely into a 2-on-1 full-court drill or a 2-on-1 half-court drill if the coach wants.

Coach Craig Kennedy
Auburn University
Auburn, Alabama

Four Corners to a Lay-up

Purpose:
To improve ballhandling, outlet and lead passes, and basic give-and-go play and lay-ups.

Organization:
You need two basketballs and a minimum of six players. Place your team in four groups, one at each foul-line extended (see diagram 1). The groups will always go diagonally. The rotation is as follows:

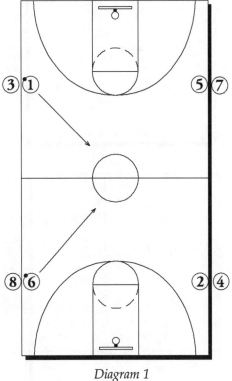

Diagram 1

1. Outlet pass to the side outlet pass, follow the pass and go to the back of the line.

2. Catch the outlet pass, make a fast-break pass or go on a transition dribble and make a lead pass.

3. Make a basket cut and lay-up (give and go).

4. After the lay-up, make an outlet pass. Follow the pass and go to the back of the line. Always outlet to the same person who gave the give-and-go pass.

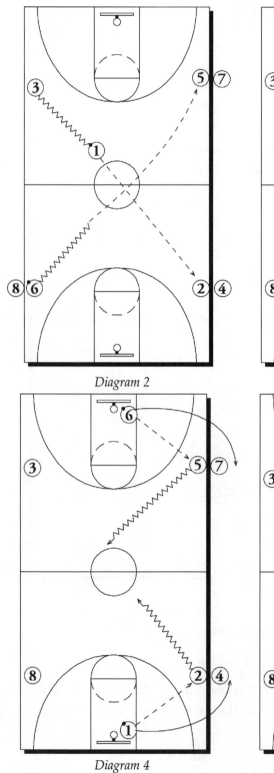

Diagram 2

Diagram 4

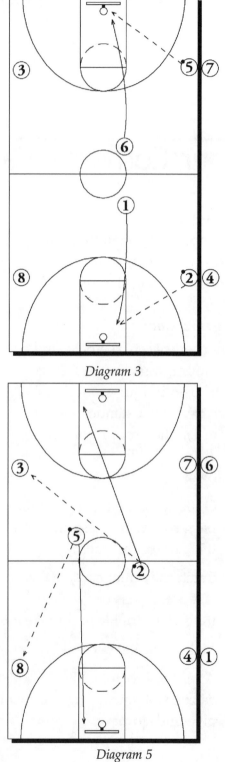

Diagram 3

Diagram 5

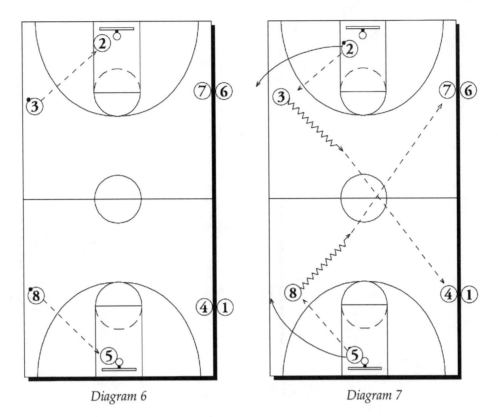

Diagram 6   Diagram 7

Start with one ball at each end of the court. Player 1 starts with the ball and advances the ball diagonally up the court either by a fastbreak pass or by taking it on the dribble then leading it ahead (diagram 2). After passing the ball, player 1 cuts to the basket for a give and go pass. Have the passers work on faking a pass first, then hitting the cutter on the block for the lay-up (diagram 3). After scoring the lay-up, player 1 takes the rebound, pivots and makes an outlet pass to player 2. Player 1 now goes to the back of the line (diagram 4). Player 2 takes the ball diagonally and leads it ahead to player 3 and then 2 cuts to the basket on the give-and-go (diagrams 5-7). Remember that the lines are always going diagonally.

While this is going on, the other group is following the same procedure in the other direction. Groups will either be doing left- or right-handed lay-ups. Always demand that they execute right-hand lay-ups on the right side and left-hand lay-ups on the left side. After reaching your goal (10 total or eight in a row), the teams switch sides of the

135

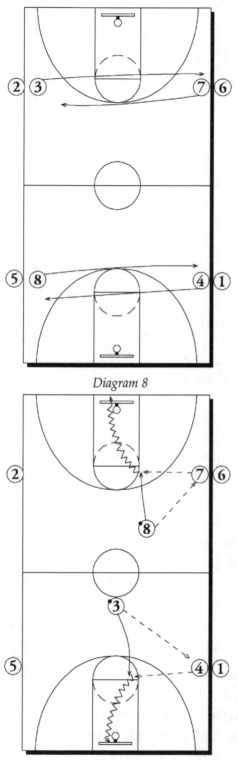

Diagram 8

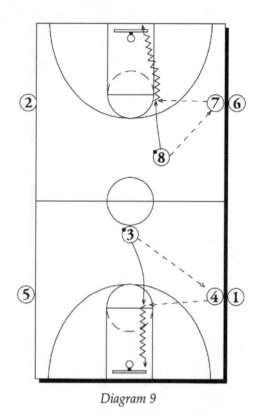

Diagram 9

Diagram 10

court to work on lay-ups with their other hand (diagram 8).

Variations include power lay-ups, reverse lay-ups, catch at the high post and execute a shot or pass fake and then drive (diagram 9), fake and cross-over (diagram 10), etc. If one end reaches their goal first, I have them work on jump shots until both ends reach their target. To increase the difficulty of this drill, have players execute a behind-the-back dribble or between-the-legs dribble, or some other dribble variation at center before they make the lead pass.

Coach Greg T. Collins
University of Louisville
Louisville, Kentucky

One-on-One Recognition Drill

Purpose:

To improve a player's ability to correctly read and execute in one on one situations.

Diagram 1

Organization:

1) Each coach begins with a ball. The drill begins with a pass and X2 closing out. O1 is permitted three dribbles, if needed, to score. After the beginning, any number of dribbles are allowed. Play continues until one of the two players score.

2) The player that scores stays on offense and a new defender enters play immediately (diagram 2).

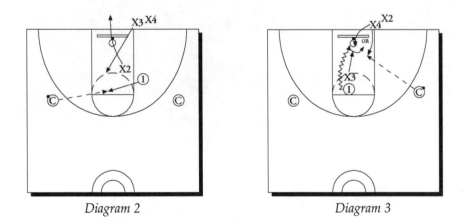

Diagram 2   *Diagram 3*

3) All shots are allowed: 3s, lay-ups, jumpshots, dunks.

4) On any made lay-up the offensive player must turn and post up the next defender under the basket (diagram 3).

5) Fouls, called by coaches, count as a made basket. A new defender enters play.

6) After scoring, the next pass must come from the other coach (alternate entry passes).

7) Keep score individually — play to a set goal of five, seven or ten points or play for a time limit on the clock.

Coaching Tips:
- Teach players how to recognize the appropriate one-on-one move to employ.

- Teach players how to get the shot they want.

Coach Greg T. Collins
University of Louisville
Louisville, Kentucky

Full Court Threes

Purpose:
To improve ballhandler's ability to execute dribble moves, pass ahead and become a scoring threat.

Organization:
1) Place a cone or defender at the three-point line in the backcourt and a cone or defender just across halfcourt. Place a chair at the elbow and a chair at the top of the key.

2) Player O1 will execute a specified dribble move at each cone, passing the ball to the coach. After completing the second move (diagram 1), the player will trail in for a return pass and spot up a three.

3) After a predetermined number of attempts or makes the ballhandler will cut to the elbow, touching the chair and popping out for a three (diagram 2).

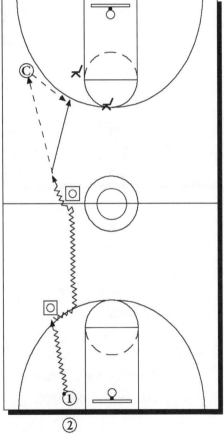

Diagram 1

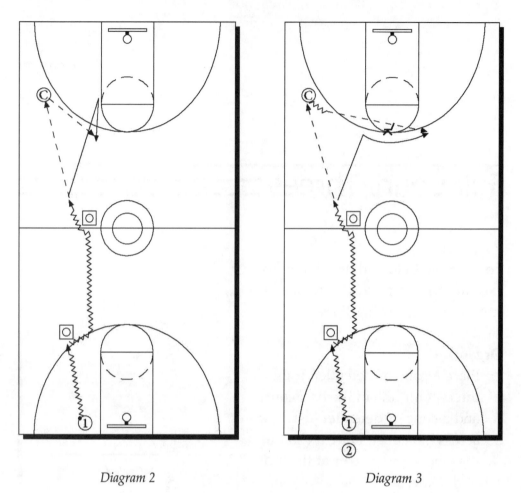

Diagram 2   *Diagram 3*

4) Again, after a pre-set number of made baskets or attempted shots, the ballhandler will execute a flare cut off the chair at the top of the screen (diagram 3).

Variations:

♦ Have the shooter get her shot, take it out and begin the drill on the other side of the court.

♦ After the shooter makes her shot, she must spring to the other side of the floor to defend the first dribble and move by the next ballhandler.

Coach John Rice
J.E. Burke High School
Dorchester, Massachusetts

Lay-up Elbow Post Shooting Drill

Purpose:
To develop shooting from different spots on the floor

Organization:
Phase One: Sprint to Lay-up
1) Player 1 sprints from the baseline to the half court and then continues running from the half court to the basket.

2) The coach passes to player 1 on the run. Player 1 catches the pass on the run and finishes with a lay-up. She then procedes to phase two.

Phase Two: Lay-up to Elbow
1) Player 1 rebounds her own shot and passes out to the coach at the top of the key.

2) Player 1 continues on to the opposite elbow for a jump shot. She must follow any misses.

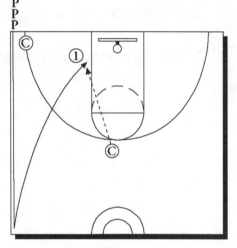

Phase 1

Phase 2

Player 1 then procedes to phase three.

Phase Three: Elbow to Post
1) Player 1 passes the rebound out to the coach in the left corner after the elbow jump shot.

2) Player 1 continues to drive to block. Player 1 receives the pass from the coach in the left corner and executes a post move. She must follow any misses.

3) Players go twice on each side.

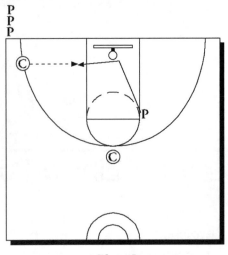

Phase 3

Coach John Rice
J.E. Burke High School
Dorchester, Massachusetts

:60 Second Shooting Drill

Purpose:
To develop speed shooting from different perimeter spots.

Organization:
  Player starts in the corner with 60 seconds on the clock. She must make three shots from each "X" spot before rotating to the next. The drill's objective is to get from corner to corner in 60 seconds.

Variation:
♦ Push the clock to 90 seconds and move the spots to outside the three-point line.

Coach Mariana O'Connor
Latin Academy High School
Boston, Massachusetts

Toss Back Shooting Series

Purpose:
To develop the proper perimeter shooting techniques off a pass.

Organization:
Phase One: Corner-Elbow Shots
1) Player 1 starts in the left corner and passes to the coach at the top of the key.

Phase 1

2) Player 1 follows the flight of the pass with her hands ready to shoot.

3) Player 1 receives a pass back from the coach at the ball-side elbow for a jump shot.

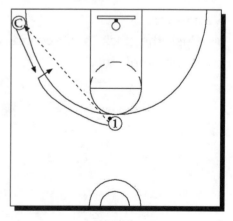

Phase Two: Top Elbow Shots
1) Player 1 starts at the top of the key and passes to the coach in the corner.

Phase 2

144

2) Player 1 follows the flight of the pass with her hands ready to shoot.

3) Player 1 receives a pass back from the coach at the ball-side elbow for a jump shot.

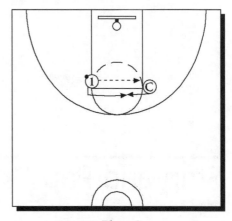

Phase 3

Phase Three: Elbow-Elbow Shots
1) Player 1 starts at the left elbow and passes to the coach at the right elbow.

2) Player 1 follows the flight of the pass with hands ready to shoot.

3) Player 1 receives a pass back from the coach at the ball-side elbow for a jump shot.

Coach Elizabeth Lawson
Clinton Christian School
Brandywine, Maryland

Stop and Pop Drill

Purpose:

To teach a team when to "stop and pop" instead of trying to make a lay-up when the option was closed.

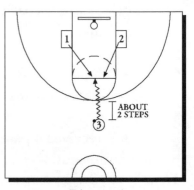

Diagram 1

Organization:

1) Players 1 and 2 are defensive players. As soon as player 3 starts to dribble, they can run up and try to block player 3's shot.

2) Player 3 starts with the ball, dribbles in as close as she can before shooting a jump shot. If player 3 has a lower skill level, she may start closer in at the three-point arc.

3) All the players rotate after each turn. Change starting position for variety (both sides).

Diagram 2

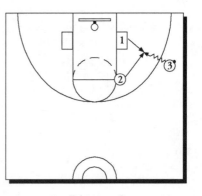

Diagram 3

Coach Bonnie Henrickson
Virginia Tech
Blacksburg, Virginia

Four Corners Drill

Purpose:
This drill emphasizes setting and using screens, as well as defending the cross-screen/down-screen.

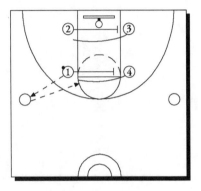

Diagram 1

Organization:
The drill consists of eight players (four offensive and four defensive) and two outlets. The outlets can be coaches and the players are not numbered according to position because each spot is interchange-able. Each time the ball is passed across the lane, there is a down-screen. Each time the ball is passed out to an outlet, there is a cross-screen. The drill involves continuous passing, screening, and moving. Each repetition can go between 20-30 seconds before switching teams. The defense is not shown.

1) The ball begins at the elbow. Player 1 can initiate the drill by throwing it out to the outlet or across to player 4. If it begins with a pass to the outlet, both ballside players cross-screen. The ball is then entered (diagram 1).

2) Player 4 then reverses the ball to player 1 and down-screens for player 3. Player 1 has the option to go back to the opposite elbow or out to the

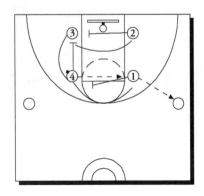

Diagram 2

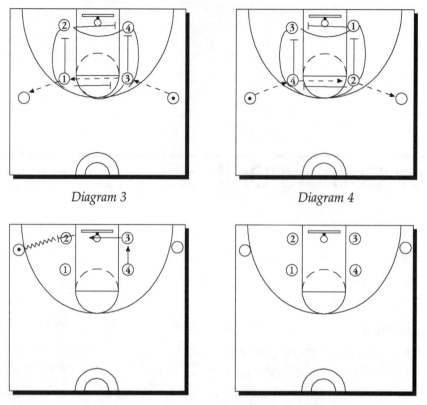

Diagram 3   Diagram 4

Diagram 5   Diagram 6

outlet. If the ball goes out to the outlet, players 1 and 2 cross-screen (diagram 2).

3) When the ball comes in to player 3, player 1 down-screens for player 2 and the ball is reversed. Once player 3 reverses the ball, she can then down-screen for player 4, giving player 2 the option of going back to the opposite elbow or out to the outlet. If the ball goes out to the outlet, players 1 and 2 cross-screen (diagram 3).

4) When the ball comes in to player 4, player 2 down-screens for player 1. The ball is then reversed to player 1 and player 4 down-screens for player 3. Player 1 has the option of going to player 3 at the elbow or out to the outlet. If the ball goes out to the outlet, Players 1 and 2 cross-screen (diagram 4).

Coaching Points:

♦ The outlets can also be placed on the baseline and are allowed to penetrate to force a weak-side rotation. Instead of using coaches as the outlets for this segment, players can be substituted (diagram 5).

♦ The down-screen can also be a back-screen (diagram 6).

Coach Jen Warden
Boise State University
Boise, Idaho

5-Ball Shooting

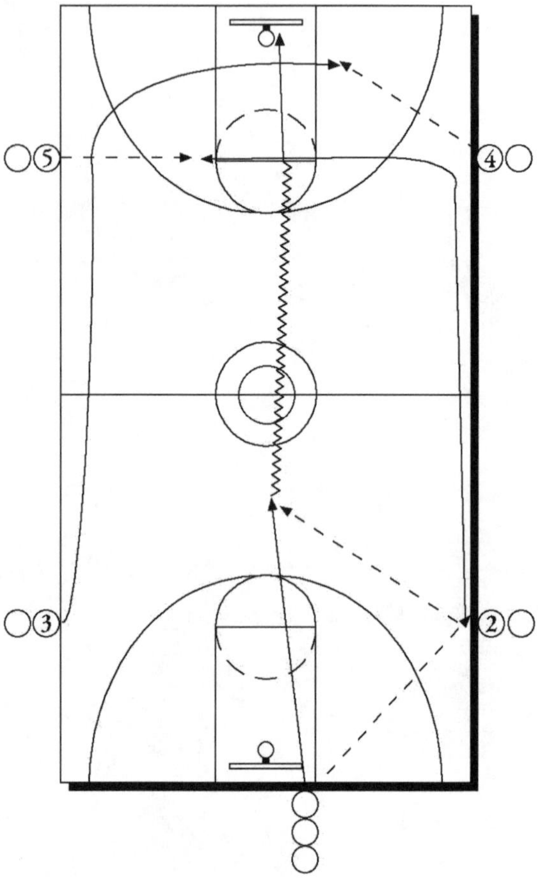

Purpose:

The objective of this drill is to improve shooting with an emphasis on shooting while tired.

Organization:

1) The drill begins with lines at the five positions shown in the diagram. O1 passes the ball to O2 and gets the ball right back. She then runs the floor for a full-court lay-up.

2) O2 and O3 run the floor on their respective sides, filling the wings. O2 goes high and receives the pass from O5, while O3 goes low and receives the pass from O4. O3 shoots from the baseline, while O4 shoots from the elbow.

3) O1 rebounds her lay-up and outlets the ball to O5. O1 gets the ball right back and shoots a lay-up.

4) O4 and O5 fill the lanes with O4 cutting low and O5 cutting high. O4 shoots from the baseline, while O5 shoots from the elbow.

Coaching Points:
Each shooter gets her own rebound and goes to the end of the line. The goal of this drill is to make 100 shots in five minutes.

CHAPTER FIVE

Transition Game: Offense and Defense

Stephen Post, Former Coach
Manhattanville College
Purchase, New York

Fast-Break Drills: Offense and Defense

Purpose:
These are a series of four drills that we use as a conditioner and warm-up usually at the beginning of practice. The drills incorporate 2-on-1 and 3-on-2 fast-break offense and defense as well as 1-on-2 and 2-on-3 press offense and defense. Each drill is done for three minutes.

Organization:
1) *Three-Drill Offense:*The players line up along the baseline as shown in diagram 1 with players 1, 4 and 7 with a ball. Player 1 dribbles the length of the floor to make a lay-up at the other end. Player 2

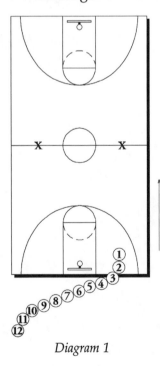

retrieves the ball and takes it out-of-bounds. If player 1 misses the lay-up, the coach has player 2 take the ball out-of-bounds or just rebound the ball and continue the ball from there. Player 3 is going to defend player 1 and try to deny the ball inbounds from player 2. The inbounds pass cannot go past the foul-line extended. Players 1 and 2 continue upcourt on a 2-on-1 fast break with player 3 defending. If player 1 missed the lay-up, the break starts immediately upon player 2 retrieving the rebound. Player 3 must get back on defense as quickly as possible. Players 1 and 2 should go as wide as possible upcourt. We place cones on the floor at mid-court to guide the players. As soon as 1, 2 and 3 finish, the next three players go (diagrams 1 & 2).

Diagram 1

154

Coaching Points: Dribble the ball as little as possible. Try to get the defense to commit to the ball before passing. Defense should try to force the offense to make a play under pressure above the foul line and not get backed up under the basket.

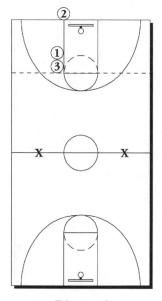

Diagram 2

2) *Three Drill Defense*: Players 1, 2 and 3 start the drill the same as in the previous drill. This time when player 2 gets the ball, players 1 and 3 attempt to trap player 2 dribbling the ball upcourt alone. Player 2 should try to get around the trap and if she can't, she should keep her dribble alive, back up, switch hands on the dribble and try to get around the other side of the trap. Split the trap only if there is a wide opening (diagram 3).

Coaching Point: Keep the dribble alive.

3) *Five Drill Offense*: Players remain in line with players 1 and 6 each having a ball. Players 1, 2 and 3 continue as in the three drill offense, with players 4 and 5 following directly behind them. Player 4 runs and touches the opposite baseline with player 5 following and then defending player 4. Player 2 may now inbound the ball to either player 1 or 4. The ball cannot be entered past the foul-line extended. After the ball gets inbounded, players 1, 2 and 4 attack on offense with players 3 and 5 on defense. Use the cones on the floor to keep the wings wide to attack the basket from the proper angle (45 degrees) after reaching the foul line extended. Players 3 and 5

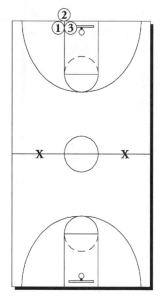

Diagram 3

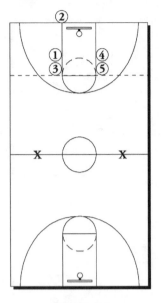

Diagram 4

retreat on defense to set up a tandem; they must communicate who will take the top and who will take the bottom. As soon as they finish, the next five go. (See Diagram 4)

Coaching Points: Get the ball to the best ball handler in the middle of the floor and use the dribble to advance the ball. Find the open shooter.

4) *Five Drill Defense*: Players 1, 2, 3, 4 and 5 start as in the previous drill. This time when player 2 takes the ball out of bounds, player 3 guards 2 with players 4 and 5 denying player 1 the ball inbounds. Player 1 must get free below the foul-line extended to get the ball. Players 1 and 2 then attack the basket versus defenders 3, 4 and 5 (see diagram 5).

Coaching Points: Keep the dribble alive. The offensive player without the ball cannot run away from her teammate. She must come back hard to the ball to help her teammate and be a receiver. She is responsible for getting open. Defense traps every pass.

These drills can also be done using groups of seven, 4-on-3 on offense and 3-on-4 on defense.

Diagram 5

3-on-2 to 3-on-3

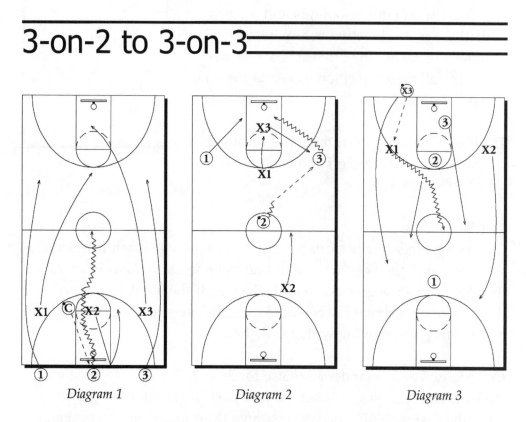

| Diagram 1 | Diagram 2 | Diagram 3 |

Purpose:
To drill transition situations both offensively and defensively.

Organization:
Start out with three offensive players on the baseline and three defensive players on the foul line facing the offense. The coach is on the foul line facing the offense with the ball. To run this drill, you will need a 30-second shot clock.

1) The coach passes to any one of the offensive players: O1, O2, O3 (diagram 1).

2) The defensive player in line with that player must run and touch the baseline as the others run a fast break down the court, 3-on-2 live (diagram 2).

3) On a score or turnover, the defensive team takes the ball out-of-bounds and pushes the ball the other direction before becoming the offensive team. The offense becomes defense and runs transition 3-on-3 to the other end (diagram 3).

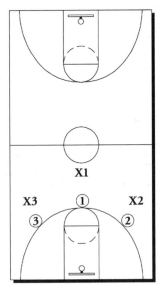

Diagram 4

4) After a team scores or there is a turnover, those two teams are off and another two are on (diagram 4).

Coaching Points:

Offensively: Stress the importance of proper spacing. Teach wings to run wide until they get to the foul line extended and then cut in above the block at a 45-degree angle to the basket. If the break is stopped, don't force up a shot. Play is 3-on-3 live, and we stress the importance of screening and moving without the ball.

Defensively: Teach a tandem defense for 3-on-2. The top player stops the ball. The back player takes the first pass. As the bottom player takes the first pass, the top players must drop to defend the basket. The defense tries to make the offense make as many passes as possible, giving their third player time to catch up.

Variation:

After the offensive team scores, have them pick up full-court defense simulating a full-court press going the other direction. The other team takes the ball out as we play 3-on-3 full court.

Coach Cheryl Dozier
University at Buffalo
Buffalo, New York

Partner Fast Break

Purpose:
Incorporates conditioning, offensive transition and finishing-on-the-break skills.

Organization:
This drill requires two players.

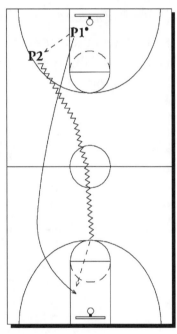

1) Player 1 throws the ball off the glass and jumps up and rebounds the ball.

2) She then outlets the ball to player 2, who immediately pushes the ball up the middle of the floor, while player 1 flies out on the wing.

3) Player 2 will jump stop at the foul line area and pass to player 1, who is driving to the basket for a lay-up. Player 1 then rebounds the ball and outlets it to player 2.

4) Players 1 and 2 return the down the floor and perform the same action, but with player 2 passing and player 1 shooting the lay-up. This pattern continues for three more trips up and down the floor. (Therefore, the pair will sprint up and down the floor for a total of eight times.)

5) The breakdown is as follows:

♦ First trip: lay-up

♦ Second trip: jump shot

♦ Third trip: pass back for a jump shot

♦ Fourth trip: give-and-go for a lay-up

Coaching Points:

♦ Again, fundamentals with conditioning are the emphasis.

♦ Make sure the player is pushing the ball hard, with head and eyes up, good jump stops, etc.

♦ It is also important that rebounder sprints up the floor and gets ahead of the person handling the ball. This will help emphasize conditioning and running the floor.

Duffy Burns, Former Coach
Cleveland State University
Cleveland, Ohio

Michigan Drill

Purpose:
To enhance the transition game with a drill that makes a player pass, catch and shoot.

Organization:
1) Player 1 passes to player 2

2) Player 2 passes to player 1

3) Player 3 sprints down the floor through the hash marks looking for the pass from player 1 to score a lay-up (diagram 1).

4) After player 1 passes to player 3, she must sprint and touch the baseline behind the shooter, because player 1 will be the shooter on the next trip.

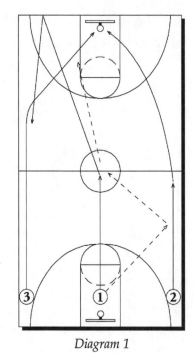

Diagram 1

5) Player 2 is the rebounder and player 3 becomes the outlet (diagram 2).

6) Player 2 rebounds made shot and passes to player 3.

7) Player 3 passes to player 2.

8) Player 1 sprints down the floor through the hash marks looking for the pass from player 2 to score the lay-up.

9) After player 2 passes to player 1, she must sprint and touch the baseline behind the shooter, because player 2 will be the shooter on the next trip.

10) Player 3 is the rebounder and player 1 becomes the outlet.

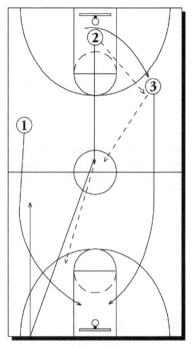

Diagram 2

Coach Joe McKeown
George Washington University
Washington, D.C.

3/2 Olympics

Purpose:
To develop transition offense and
defense skills.

Organization:

1) Players X1, 2 and 3 attack 3-2
   against players X4 and X5.

2) X4 and X5 rebound and outlet to
   X6, then continue 3-2 full court.

3) Continue for five to eight minutes.

4) The two wings and offense become
   the defense after they shoot.

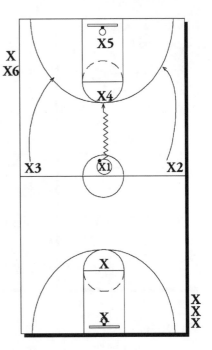

Duffy Burns, Former Coach
Cleveland State University
Cleveland, Ohio

Perfection Drill

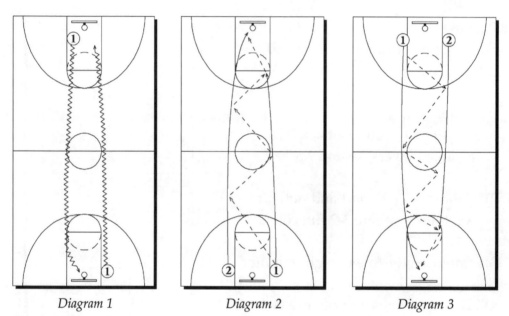

| Diagram 1 | Diagram 2 | Diagram 3 |

Purpose:

To enhance transition game with a drill that makes players pass, catch, run and shoot continuously. This drill also improves concentration.

Organization:

There are five levels of perfection:
1) Full-court lay-up
2) Box-to-box lay-up
3) Same-side lay-up
4) Three-player weave — lay-up
5) Three-player weave — jumper

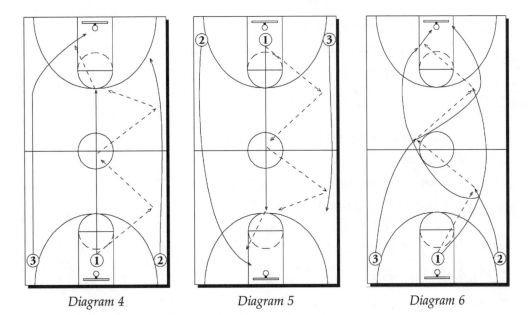

| Diagram 4 | Diagram 5 | Diagram 6 |

1) *Full-court lay-up* (diagram 1)
   a) Right-hand lay-up at both ends of the floor.
   b) Use alternating dribbles and try to use no more than seven dribbles total
   c) When the first player gets to half court, then the next player goes.

2) *Box-to-box lay-up* (diagram 2)
   a) Players 1 and 2 pass back and forth.
   b) Call box-to-box at half court.
   c) Player 1 jump stops at elbow and player 2 shoots the lay-up.
   d) Player 1 rebounds the lay-up and player 2 becomes the outlet.
   e) Use no more than five passes on each trip.
   f) Players 2 and 1 pass back and forth (diagram 3).
   g) Call box-to-box at half court.
   h) Player 2 jump stops at elbow and player 1 shoots the lay-up.
   i) Next group goes.

3) *Same side lay-up* (diagram 4)
   a) Players 1 and 2 pass back and forth on the right side of the floor.
   b) Player 3 sprints down the floor through the hash marks, looking for the pass from player 1 to score the lay-up.

c) Player 1 rebounds the made lay-up, player 3 becomes the outlet and player 2 becomes the shooter on the next trip.

d) Use no more than five passes on each trip.

e) Players 1 and 3 pass back and forth (diagram 5).

f) Player 2 sprints down the floor through the hash marks, looking for the pass from player 1 to score the lay-up.

g) Next group goes.

4) *Three-player weave — lay-up* (diagram 6)

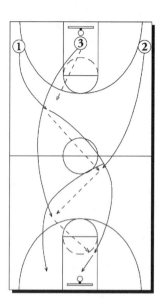

Diagram 7

5) *Three-player weave —jumper*

a) Player 1 passes to player 2 and cuts behind.

b) Player 2 passes to player 3 and cuts behind.

c) Player 3 passes to player 1 and cuts behind.

d) Player 1 passes to player 2 for lay-up.

e) Player 3 rebounds made lay-up and player 1 becomes outlet.

f) Player 3 passes to player 1 and cuts behind (diagram 7).

g) Player 1 passes to player 2 and cuts behind.

h) Player 2 passes to player 3 and cuts behind.

i) Player 3 passes to player 1 for lay-up.

j) Next group goes.

In level five, use the same procedure as used in level four, except that the shooter should jump stop on the wing for a jumper. If a jumper is missed, just follow up the miss.

Coaching Notes:
◆ Every player goes at least once in each level.
◆ The player must score at both ends in each level.
◆ There can be no ballhandling or passing errors.
◆ Each player must use the glass on all lay-ups.
◆ The drill must be done at full speed.
◆ Everything must be perfect or the player must repeat that level.

Nancy Lieberman
Naismith Memorial Basketball Hall of Fame
Pepsi/Nancy Lieberman Basketball Camps
Carrollton, Texas

3-on-2 Chaser

Purpose:
To develop the decision-making abilities of the point guard.

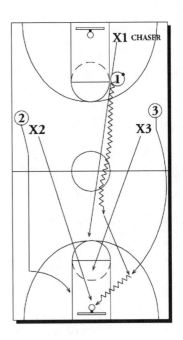

Organization:
The drill is run as a 3-on-3 with a defensive chaser. The point guard gets a 15-foot head start on the chaser who is starting on the baseline. The other two defenders are just inside their respective players two steps closer to their defensive basket. On the whistle, the point guard pushes the ball 3-on-2 with the chaser trailing the play. Communication is essential for the defense to keep the offense from scoring.

Variation:
The drill can be used as a team competition drill. Six players are needed on each team. After the first group goes, the next six players step on. The drill is then repeated. After the second group goes, the teams switch offense to defense. Score is kept throughout, with the game ending with either a predetermined possession limit or specific time allotted.

Coach Charlene Curtis
Wake Forest University
Winston-Salem, North Carolina

3-on-3 Full Court Score and Defend

Purpose:

To improve offense and defense concepts in
game conditions.

Organization:

Rules in the Backcourt:

♦ Offense may not dribble.

♦ Offense must position herself between the
ball and the defender.

♦ Offense may not use screens

♦ Offense must cut on a straight (vertical) line
toward the ball in order to receive a pass.
Cuts may be on an angle but never horizon-
tal.

♦ Offense may use post swim move techniques
and post-up to gain advantage versus defense.

♦ Passes may not be made over the defender's
head.

♦ Defense must stand within two feet of the
offense in a full face denial. (Defense has her
back to the ball.)

Diagram 1

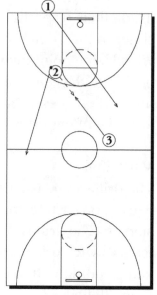

Diagram 2

1) Player 1 inbounds the ball to player 2. Player
   1 is permitted to run the baseline. Player 2 goes away then cuts back to
   the ball through the defender. Player 3 goes away to create good

spacing. If player 2 did not get open for pass from player 1, player 3 cuts back to the ball (diagram 1).

2) Player 2 passes to player 3 who has cut back to the ball through her defender. Player 1 goes away to create good spacing. If player 3 did not get open for a pass from player 2, player 1 cuts back to the ball (diagram 2).

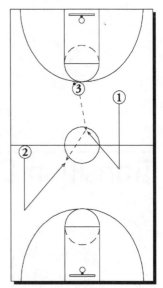

Rules in the Frontcourt:

◆ Offense and defense use fundamental basketball techniques for 3-on-3 basketball play.

◆ Offense is permitted to screen and dribble. (Coach may limit offense's options.)

Diagram 3

◆ Defense uses man principles as directed by coach.

◆ If offense scores, defense now becomes offense and follows backcourt rules going to the opposite basket. Offense becomes defense.

3) Player 3 passes to 1 who has cut back to the ball. Then player 1 passes to 2 who cuts back to the ball. When the ball is caught in the frontcourt, the offense may now screen and dribble. The defense plays good half-court man defense as directed by the coach (diagram 3).

The goal is to score and then prevent the opponent from scoring on consecutive possessions. Drill continues until team A or team B scores, then successfully defends on consecutive possessions. If team A scores then successfully defends, team A goes out of the drill. A new three-player team steps on the court as defense versus team B.

Benefits of Score and Defend Drill:
◆ Teaches offensive players to move without the ball.
◆ Teaches offensive change-of-direction moves.
◆ Teaches passing and catching versus pressure defense.
◆ Provides opportunity to teach half-court 3-on-3 offense and defense. Coach determines the half-court emphasis.
◆ Emphasizes the importance of getting a defensive stop in crucial game situations.

Coach Jill M. Pizzotti
Saint Louis University
St. Louis, Missouri

Transition Drill

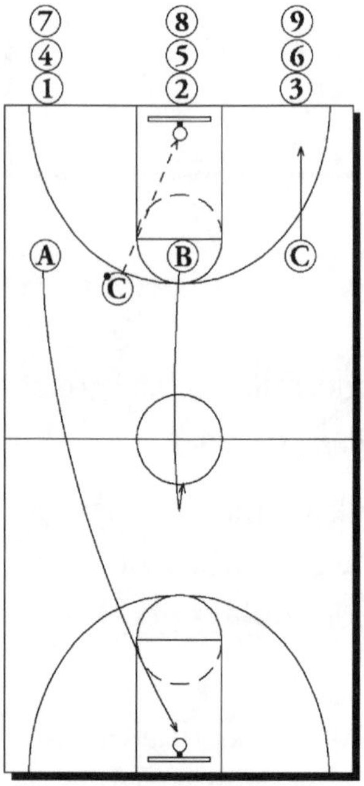

| Diagram 1 | Diagram 2 | Diagram 3 |

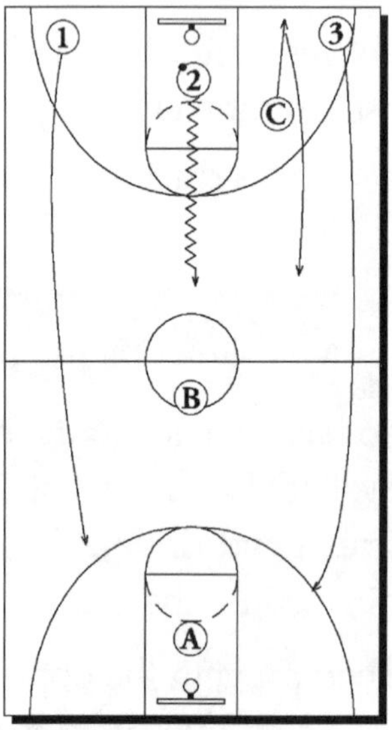

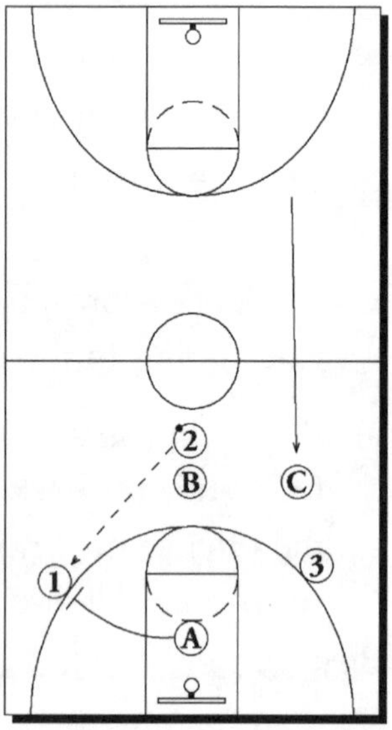

Purpose:
To teach transition defense.

Organization:
1) The coach calls the name of a defensive player. In this example, player "C" (diagram 1).

2) The coach passes the ball to any one of the three offensive players on the baseline. In this example, 2. At this time, player C sprints to the baseline and then to the defensive end of the floor while play-

ers A and B are sprinting to the defensive end of the floor. One must guard the ball, the other the first pass. In this example, B is guarding the ball and A takes the first pass (diagram 2).

3) Player C comes in the play as quickly as possible (diagram 3).

Coaching Point:
Basically, the drill starts 3-on-2, and then becomes 3-on-3. The defenders learn to communicate. The offense learns to make quick decisions in transition. Can also run drill 4-on-4.

Coach John Ishee
Life University
Marietta, Georgia

Defensive Transition Drill

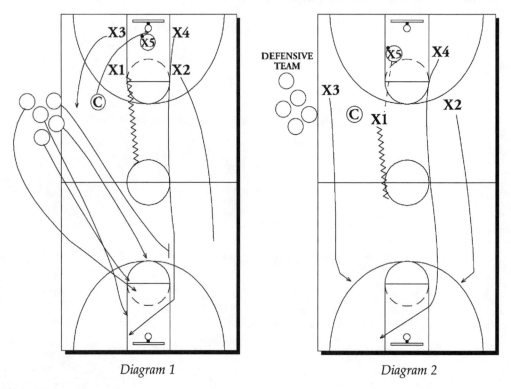

Diagram 1   *Diagram 2*

Purpose:
To improve defense transition skills.

Organization:
Although this drill looks like mass confusion, it is really very simple!

1) A coach puts up a shot and one of the players rebounds it, in this diagram, it is player 5 (diagram 1).

2) The player then brings the ball as quickly as possible with the dribble, two others fill the quickest lanes possible and the last player trails — that's the rebounder (diagram 2).

3) The defensive team from the side cannot leave until the rebounder outlets the ball (diagram 3).

Defensive Goals:

1) Stop the ball.

2) Take away inside options.

3) Take away all ball-side options.

4) Close out/block out and give up no second shots!

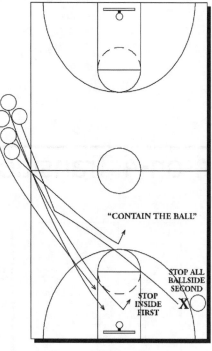

Diagram 3

173

4-on-4 Transition D

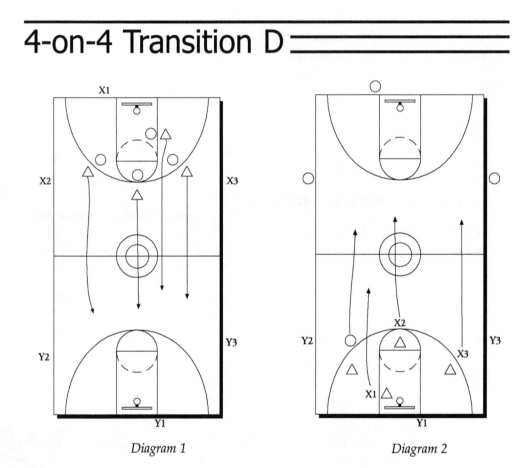

Diagram 1   *Diagram 2*

Purpose:

The objective of this drill is to improve transition defense and communication skills.

Organization:

1) The drill begins with a 4-on-4 set on one end of the court. There is a player on each baseline (X1, Y1) and on both sidelines of each half-court end around the top of the key (X2, X3, Y2, Y3).

174

2) On a change of possession, all four players that were on offense will sprint to the other end and play defense. The two players on the sidelines are looking to get the outlet pass and will attack the basket at the opposite end, and the baseline player sprints to play offense.

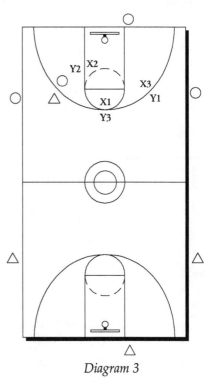

Diagram 3

3) Of the four players that were initially playing defense, one player will outlet to either of the players on the sidelines and will play offense with them (this will be the player who gets a steal, a defensive rebound, or is the closest to the ball when it goes through the net).

4) The three remaining players that were on offense will then fill the spots left vacant (sidelines/baselines). The sequence will continue for 8-10 minutes with stoppage of play to talk about situations.

1-on-1 to 5-on-5

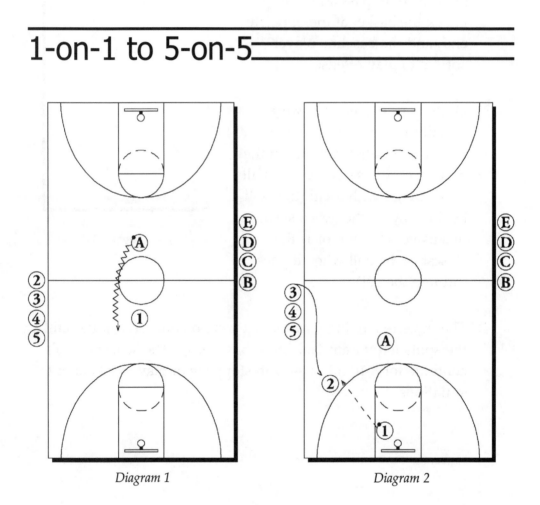

Diagram 1   Diagram 2

Purpose:
To improve 1-on-1, transition offense and defense, man advantage and disadvantage situations and half-court play and full-court play.

Organization:
Divide the team into two squads and place them on opposite sides of the court at the center line. Set a goal of total points or a time limit for

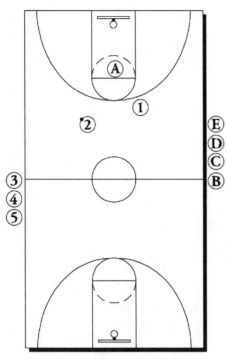

Diagram 3

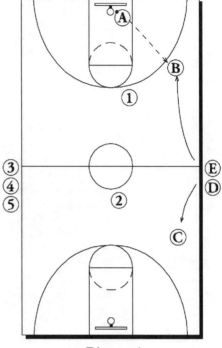

Diagram 4

this exercise. The drill can begin by a jump ball, loose ball or make it, take it.

Start out with a 1-on-1 situation. In diagram 1, player A has the ball on offense first. As soon as player 1 takes possession of the ball (rebound, turnover, score) teammate 2 comes on and goes to the outlet spot (diagram 2). The drill is now 2-on-1 (diagram 3). As soon as A's team gets the ball, the two teammates B and C come on. B is the outlet and C can go long (diagram 4). The drill is now 3-on-2 (diagram 5). When 1 and 2 get the ball, they are joined by 3 and 4

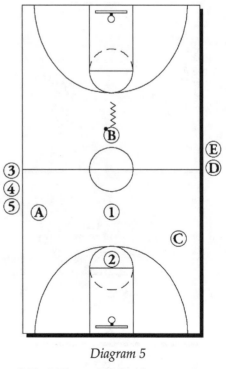

Diagram 5

to make the drill 4-on-3 (diagrams 6 and 7). When ABC take posses-

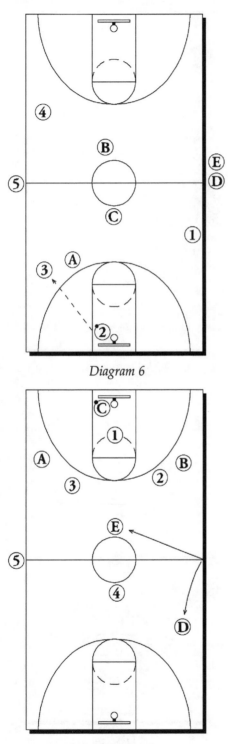

Diagram 6

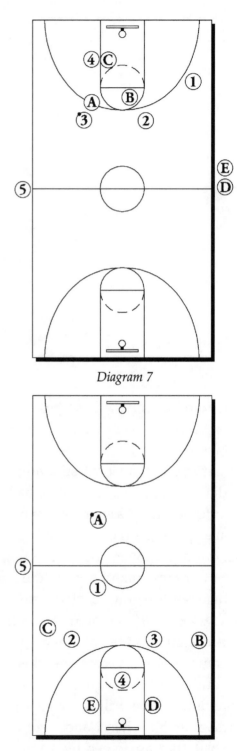

Diagram 7

Diagram 8

Diagram 9

sion, they are joined by D and E to make the drill 5-on-4 (diagrams 8 and 9). When 1 2 3 4 get the ball, 5 joins in to make it 5-on-5 (diagram 10).

After the 5-on-5 situation, you can stop and start over at 1-on-1 or add more players to increase the pressure by going on to a 6-on-5 situation. The drill follows with adding one player on the first change of possession, two players on the second, third and fourth possession, and add one player on the last possession.

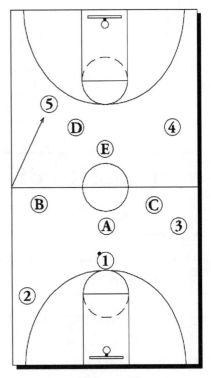

Diagram 10

Coach Kevin Pigott
Fordham Prep School
Bronx, New York

Transition Fast Break

Purpose:
To develop offensive ball movement and defensive transition in both the half-court and full-court.

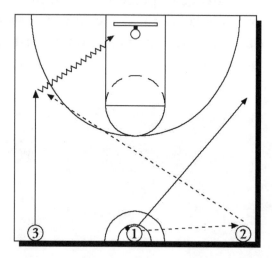

Organization:
1) *Phase One: Three-on-Zero (Half-Court):*
   a) Player 1 starts at center court with the ball. Player 2 is on the right wing. Player 3 is on the left wing.

   b) Player 1 passes to player 2 and sprints to player 2's sideline. Player 3 sprints to the opposite sideline.

   c) Player 2 now passes to player 3 for a lay-up.

Variation:
If two defenders are added, limit the offense to two dribbles and two passes.

2) *Phase Two: Three-on-Three (Full Court)*
   a) Players 1, 2 and 3 start lined up across the baseline. Players X1, X2 and X3 line up across from each offensive player at the free throw line and extended. The coach has the ball (anywhere) and passes to any offensive player.

180

b) The defender of the offensive player who receives the pass must run and touch the baseline.

c) Players 1, 2 and 3 run their fast break as the remaining two defenders get back in transition.

d) Offensive Rules: Get the ball to the middle to a ballhandler and get up the floor (wide).

e) Defensive Rules: Get back in transition to protect the basket and stop the ball. The trailing defender must get back in the open area.

Variation:

Use a point system at both ends. For example, offensive scoring: two points for a field goal, three points for a three-pointer, one point for an offensive rebound and one point for a shooting foul; defensive scoring: one point each for rebounding, stopping or deflecting the ball. Air ball and match-up before a shot is one point. A steal is two points and three points for a charge.

Coach Greg T. Collins
University of Louisville
Louisville, Kentucky

One or Two Speed Lay-ups

Purpose:

To improve a player's ability to handle the ball at a fast pace and finish a lay-up under pressure. To improve the defender's abilty to sprint back on defense to stop uncontested lay-ups without fouling.

Organization:

1) Player O1 begins just across the half-court line. Player X1 begins just behind the half-court line between the coach and O1. X2 begins opposite O1.

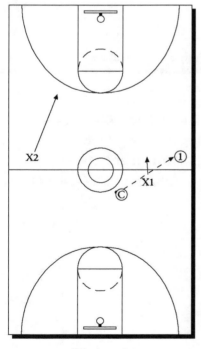

Diagram 1

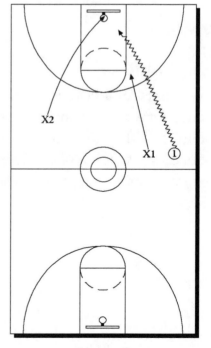

Diagram 2

2) The drill begins as the coach passes to O1. X1 and X2 cannot move until the pass is made (diagram 1). As O2 catches the ball, she puts it on the floor trying to beat X1 and X2, scoring a second lay-up (diagram 2).

3) Make or miss, O1 will sprint back on defense and X1 and X2 will become offensive players in a 2-on-1 break to the other end (diagram 3).

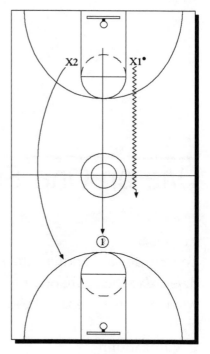

Diagram 3

Coach Greg T. Collins
University of Louisville
Louisville, Kentucky

One-on-One Sprint Under

Purpose:
To improve a) handling the ball under pressure; b) applying pressure defense to the ballhandler and c) sprinting under the level of the ball whenever it is passed ahead.

Organization:
1) The drill begins with O1 getting open for the inbounds pass. Then X1 turns the ballhandler until getting it stopped (diagram 1).

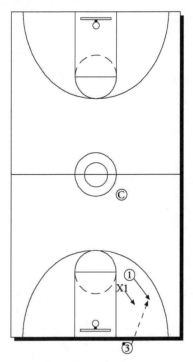

Diagram 1

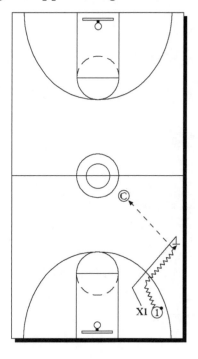

Diagram 2

2) Once the ballhandler picks up the ball, she passes ahead to the coach (diagram 2). Player X1 should sprint as soon as the ball is passed, sprinting below the level of the ball always seeing O1.

3) As O1 enters the front court, the coach returns the ball to O1. X1 closes out and they play one-on-one. Change offense and defense, return and repeat the drill.

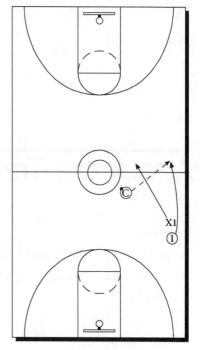

Diagram 3

Coach Greg T. Collins
University of Louisville
Louisville, Kentucky

Attack the Trap Using the Dribble

Purpose:

To improve player's abilty to beat a trap, using dribble moves and decision-making skills. To improve defensive player's ability to trap a live ball.

Organization:

1) The court is divided into four areas. X1 will defend the inbound pass in section four. X2 and X3 will trap only in section three. X4

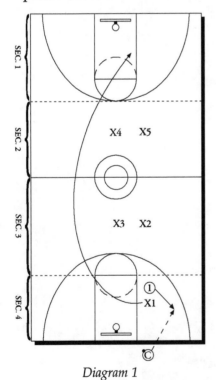

Diagram 1

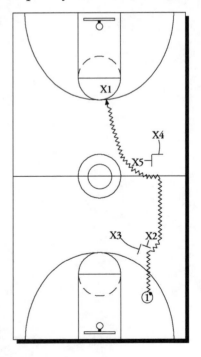

Diagram 2

186

and X5 will trap only in section two. X1 will sprint to defend the basket after the inbounds pass is complete (diagram 1).

2) X2 and X3 will try to trap O1 in section three. O1 can go any-where in the backcourt, but she must not get a 10 second viola-tion (diagram 2).

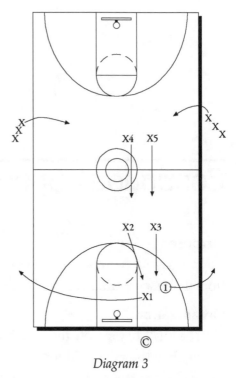

3) After beating the first tap, O1 must attack and beat the second trap. Then she will meet X1 again and beat her with a one-on-one move to score. Change offense/defense and return.

Diagram 3

Coach Greg T. Collins
University of Louisville
Louisville, Kentucky

Continuous Speed Lay-ups

Purpose:

To improve a ballhandler's speed and control in a breakaway situation. To teach pursuing the ballhandler for a backtip or strip.

Organization:

1) The drill begins on the coach's outlet pass to O1. As player 1 catches the pass, player 3 takes off trying to force a turnover, get a backtip if the ball is dribbled with the inside hand or strip the ball as the shooter goes up for a lay-up (diagram 1).

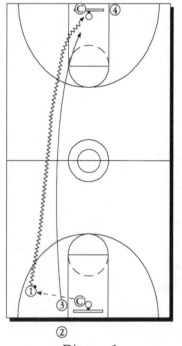

Diagram 1

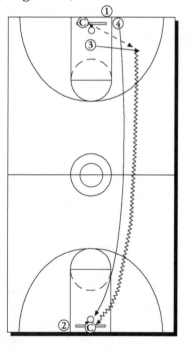

Diagram 2

2) The drill continues as the coach gets the ball and outlets it to player 3. Player 4 is ready to pursue the ball on the catch (diagram 2).

3) The drill continues until a number of lay-ups are made, attempted or stopped.

Variation:
Have the offensive player become the defensive pursuer immediately after the made lay-up instead of having defense waiting.

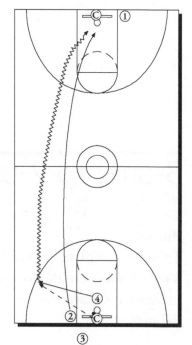

Diagram 3

Coach Tara VanDerveer
Stanford University
Stanford, California

3-on-2 to 2-on-1

Purpose:

This drill emphasizes both offensive and defensive skills. Passing and 3-on-2 breaks are the focus on offense. Defending the fast break and hedging back and forth while protecting the basket are the focus on defense.

Organization:

Three lines are formed on the baseline and two defensive players are positioned at the other end of the court, as shown in the diagram.

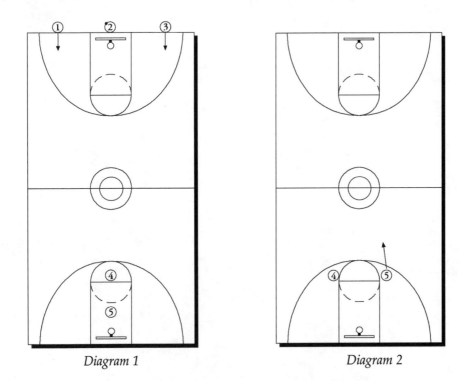

Diagram 1   Diagram 2

1) 1, 2, and 3 weave to half-court, then take it against 4 and 5, trying to get a lay-up or short jumper without over passing. Player 4 stops the ball while player 5 has the first pass to either wing. Player 4 then drops and protects the basket.

2) After 4 and 5 get the rebound, or get the ball out of the net, they bring the ball down against whoever shot the ball (1, 2, or 3). Players 4 and 5 again are trying to get a lay-up or short jumper. The defense should hedge back and forth, protecting the basket.

CHAPTER SIX

Rebounding Drills

Allison Greene, Former Coach
Old Dominion University
Norfolk, Virginia

Arcs and Angles

| Baseline | Wing | 3-point Circle |

Purpose:
This drill is all about physics. It is designed to improve both offensive and defensive rebounding.

Organization:
Begin with two players — one is shooting, one is rebounding. The intent is to train the eye to anticipate where a missed shot may fall. This is done by observing the following things:

1. *Distance*: the rebounder takes into account the distance from whence the shooter is shooting. (For example, longer shots result in longer rebounds, etc.)

2. *Arc*: the rebounder watches the flight of the ball to observe the arc of the ball. (For example, the higher the arc, the softer the shot off the rim and the closer it will fall to the rim, etc.)

3. *Angle*: the spot on the floor where the shot originated from is at a certain angle to the basket. If the shot misses, one can anticipate the

most likely place the rebound will occur. (For example, a missed shot on the baseline will typically bounce to the opposite baseline, or right back to the shooter, whereas a missed shot taken at a 45 degree angle will typically miss at a 45 degree angle to the other side of the key, etc.)

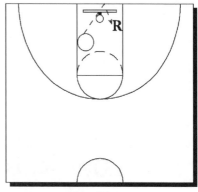

Close Distance

Have your team partner up and rebound for each other. The shooter should take multiple shots from varied spots on the floor. As the shooter is shooting, say 20 shots from the same distance on the right baseline, the rebounder is taking note of what that teammate's shot looks like in the air a) when it goes in the hole and b) when it misses. Eventually, the rebounder gets better at anticipating a missed shot's typical location and can move in the direction of where the ball may go. On a missed shot, the rebounder must grab the offensive board and finish the shot. This is done at game speed.

Over time, as partners are rotated and teammates rebound for all other team members, the desired result is better rebounding anticipation skills. While the more specific and individualized styles of your opponents are less familiar, one can still better approximate the most likely place a missed shot will occur. Sometimes, it is helpful for your team to take a few minutes to observe the other team's shooting styles during the time teams are casually shooting (before the structured 20 minute warm-up period). One can observe scouting films as well. Watch the players who take the most shots, in particular. In comparison to past seasons, take note of your overall offensive rebounding average to see if it increases with the implementation of this drill in practice. You will notice that the best rebounders (at all levels of the game) already utilize the above methods instinctively.

Note: These diagrams are simple examples to show where the rebounder would be in anticipation of a missed shot.

J. Carol Ross, Former Coach
University of Florida
Gainesville, Florida

High-Low Rebounding

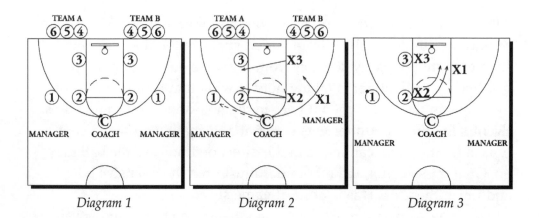

Diagram 1   Diagram 2   Diagram 3

Purpose:
This drill works on shooting, boxing out and rebounding in a competitive atmosphere.

Orgnization:
Divide players into two teams. They can split by first team vs. second team, posts vs. guards, younger players vs. older players, etc.

1) Each team occupies the three spots on the court (diagram 1).

2) The coach throws the ball to the shooter (1) on team A. Players 2 and 3 must post and roll for the ball. (They are penalized one point if they do not.) X2 and X3 must assume defensive positions. (They are penalized one point if they do not.) X1 prepares to rebound on the weak side (diagram 2).

3) Player 1 shoots (3-point shot unless coach restricts range for particular shooters) and follows shot. Player 3 rebounds strong side with X3 boxing out. Player 2 rebounds weak side with X2 boxing out. X2 rebounds to the weak side. If offense rebounds, play until scored (defense matches up) or defense rebounds. If defense rebounds, outlet to manager (diagram 3).

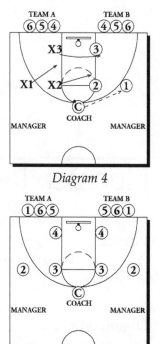

Diagram 4

4) Repeat with coach passing to team B. Team B is now on offense (diagram 4).

5) Drill continues alternating sides with each shooter shooting two shots before rotating (diagram 5).

Diagram 5

Coaching Points:

1) Play for four minutes, keeping time and score on the clock.

2) Scoring as follows:
   Made 2- or 3-point shot: 1 point
   Offensive rebound: 1 point
   Defensive rebound: 1 point
   Shooting foul: 1 point
   Players 2 and 3 don't post/call for ball: -1 point
   X2 and X3 don't defend players 2 and 3 before rebounding: -1 point

Coach Belinda "Boe" Pearman
University of Rhode Island
Kingston, Rhode Island

Monster Rebounding

Purpose:
Focus on physical play with the ability
to finish the shot.

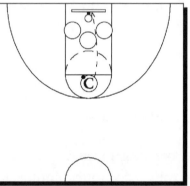

Organization:
The drill starts with the coach and three
to four players at a basket.

1) The players are moving around. The
   coach throws the ball off the
   backboard, and the players scramble to gain possession of the ball.

2) The player that gets the ball tries to score against the other players
   — she may NOT dribble.

3) Only limited fouls are called — none in most cases.

4) After scoring, drill begins again with coach's toss.

5) The winner is the first player to score five buckets.

Coach Kay Yow
North Carolina State University
Raleigh, North Carolina

2-on-2 Rebounding

Purpose:
To drill both offensive and defensive rebounding techniques.

Organization:
This drill requires 12 players and one ball. Six players are positioned at the foul line, three at each elbow facing the basket. They are on offense. The other six are positioned under the basket in two lines. They begin as the defense. Rotation of lines is based on who scores. One of the defensive lines starts the drill by making a pass to one of the offensive lines. There is no out-of-bounds in this drill. Everything is inbounds.

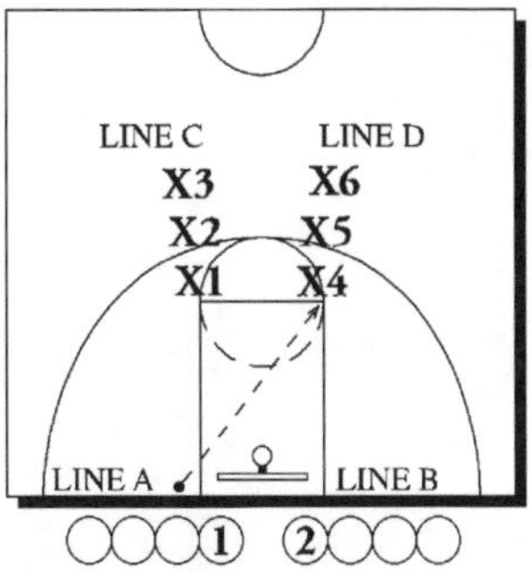

Diagram 1

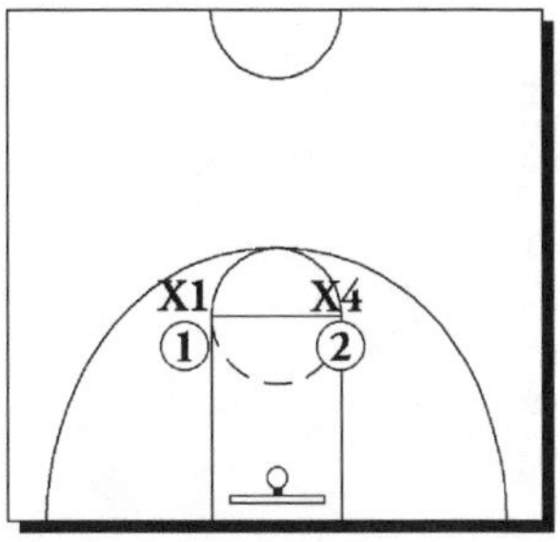

Diagram 2

The ball starts in line A or B. The player passes the ball to line C or D. (The shot clock is started with 20 seconds on it when the first shot is taken.) The player in line C or D shoots as lines A and B contest shot and box out at the elbows. Play is now live regardless of whether a shot is made or missed, and all four players try to box each other out and rebound the ball. The team that rebounds the ball tries to score and play is live, 2-on-2. Both teams continue to try to box out and rebound on shots until there is a score. The team that scores fills in lines A and B. The losers go to the top, filling lines C and D. After a three-five minute time period, players in line C and D run a sprint.

199

Coaching Points:

1) Stress the importance of boxing out and staying with the play. Teach players to be aggressive and to go up strong.

2) Box out on short shots as well as long shots.

3) Offensively, don't be a stationary target. Move and counter the defensive box out to get to the ball.

4) This should be an intense fast-moving drill. If a foul occurs, fouling team is off and goes to line C or D and the team that was fouled is off and goes to lines A and B.

Karen Hall, Former Coach
North Carolina A&T State University
Greensburg, North Carolina

Rebound-Outlet-Middle Drill

Purpose:
To improve rebound and outlet passing. Initiate the fast break.

Organization:

1) The rebounder outlets the ball to the player on wing. Rebounder fills right lane.

2) The outlet passes the ball to the middle player sprinting to center. Run and fill left lane.

3) The middle dribbles to the free-throw line and passes ball right to left for shooter.

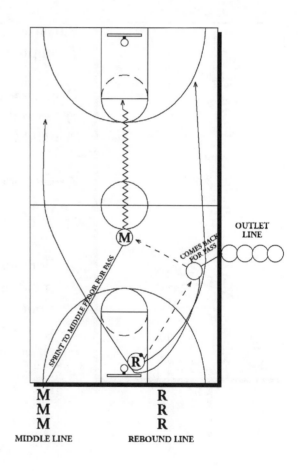

201

Coach Kathy Warner Corbett
Oglethorpe University
Atlanta, Georgia

Team Rebounding

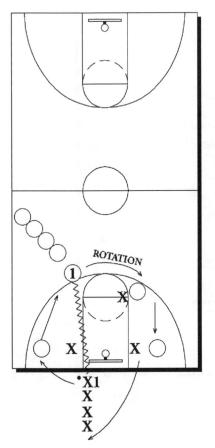

Purpose:
To improve team rebounding.

Organization:
1) X1 rolls ball to O1 and follows to defend O1.

2) O1 shoots upon receiving the ball.

3) Defensive team blocks out.

4) Both teams go hard for the rebound. If offense gets the rebound, they continue trying to score. Once defense gets rebound, X and O rotate one position to the right.

Coach Kevin L. Allen
West Florence High School
Florence, South Carolina

"21" Rebound Drill

Purpose:
To get players more involved in the
aspect of rebounding. This employs the
actions of offensive and defensive
rebounding skills. This drill can be
performed for a complete team or
merely the post players on your team.

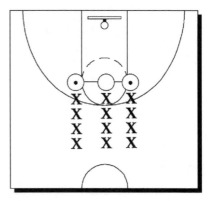

Organization:
Three balanced lines are established.
There are lines at each elbow and one in the middle at the free-throw
line. A basketball is placed at the front of the two lines at the elbow.
The middle line will not recieve a ball.

On the signal the two lines with basketballs will shoot from their line
position. The middle line that does not have a ball will work for defensive rebound position to gain possession of a ball. If the individual
from the middle line does get a rebound she can stick it back in for a
point. When a shot is made, regardless if from the line or on a stick-
back, the person that shot the ball must get a rebound and pass the
ball back to her line. If the shot is missed, the ball must be rebounded
and put back in. Any shot made from the line position is worth 2
points. Any rebound stick-back is worth one point.

There is always going to be a player without a ball. Once the balls are
shot at the beginning there is a battle for each rebound and stick-back.
The first team to get to 21 points is the winner with the other two performing the extra skill of the coaches' choice while the winners sit out.

Coach Eric L. Stratman
Quincy Senior High School
Quincy, Illinois

Group Rebounding Drills ===

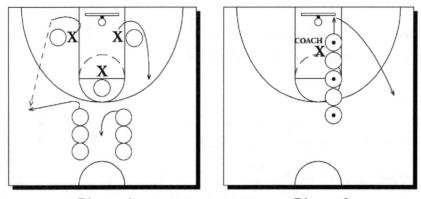

Diagram 1   *Diagram 2*

Purpose:
To improve team rebounding skills.

Organization:
1) *Meatgrinder Drill:* The coach shoots with the rebound rim in place. Three players on defense block out, board and outlet. Their starting positions may be varied.

   Two guards, upon seeing rebound, angle out to recieve outlet. the nonreceiving guard fills middle and non-rebounding forward fills outside. Allow fouling, but no biting.

   Two defenders wait at the opposite end to complete 3-on-2 break (diagram 1).

Variations:
♦ Eliminate fast-break part of drill to emphasize the board work.
♦ Use 4-on-4, 5-on-5, to start the drill.

2) *Outlet Pass Drill:* Every other player in line along lane starts with a ball. The ball is put up on boards and then that player clears out to receive outlet pass.

The next player in line rebounds the ball and clears out to the 38-foot line. A coach usually fights each rebound and outlet.

Squad stays on the drill until 25 "good ones" are had from each side of the board (diagram 2).

Coach Keith Holubesko
Five-Star Basketball Camp
Yonkers, New York

The Rebound Game

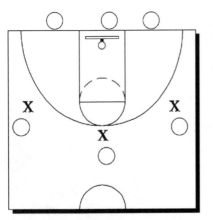

Purpose:
To improve defensive rebounding skills.

Organization:
The drill setup begins with three offensive players and three defensive players on the perimeter. Under the basket are three lines that are for other players in teams of three waiting to rotate in the drill. The drill starts with the coach blowing the whistle. Once the whistle is blown, the offensive players pass the ball around the perimeter while the defense works on defensive positioning only. When the whistle is blown again, the offensive player with the ball shoots. The players on defense first yell "shot" to inform their team that a shot has been taken. The second verbal is "box," which tells the defensive players to box out their offensive opponents. The game is played to five points. The first team to reach five wins. The only way to get a point is to obtain a rebound on defense. Therefore, the rotation of the drill is that the team that does not get a rebound gets out of the drill, the team that got the rebound goes to defense or stays on defense, and the team waiting comes in on offense always. Be aware that some players may cheat by running in without boxing out. If so, then take away their turn. The game is usually played until one team is left and usually they are made to run some kind of conditioner.

Coach Dave Odom
University of South Carolina
Columbia, South Carolina

Rebounding Drills

Purpose:

To improve offensive and defensive rebounding skills.

Organization:

Points to remember to become a good rebounder:

Defensive Rebounding

a) When a shot goes up, find your player and make contact outside the lane

b) Make contact with the forearm, then butt

c) Knees bent with hands up and elbows out

d) Pursue the ball; be the reactor

e) Grab the ball with two hands

f) Chin the ball

Offensive Rebounding

a) Be active; go every time

b) Try to get inside your player and then block her out; if you can't get inside, get beside; if you can't do either, push her under the basket

c) Don't lean on the player blocking you out; use your feet to create space and get around

d) "Attitude is everything" – every shot is a pass to you

e) If you can't rebound the ball, tip it out to keep it alive

f) If you are fronted, sprint to the weakside on the shot

1) *Warm-up*

   a) Rim Touches: Jump off two feet and touch the rim or a certain spot on the wall for 45 seconds, then repeat. Make sure you

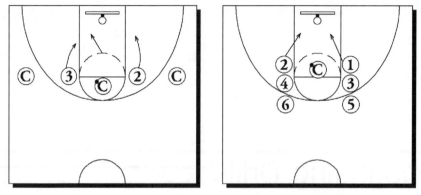

Diagram 1   Diagram 2

keep both arms high and as soon as your feet hit the floor, jump again (be a quick jumper).

b) *Outlet Rebounding:* Throw the ball off the boards; rebound the ball with two hands. Chin the ball then pivot to the outside and outlet the ball. Do this continuously for one minute.

2) *Offensive Rebounding Drill:* Player 1 is facing the coach, chopping her feet. The coach shoots, player 1 pivots and rebounds the ball. Players 2 and 3 must wait until the ball hits the rim. Then they go hard to the ball and try to strip it from player 1. Player 1 must make the outlet pass (diagram 1).

3) *Two Man Offensive Rebounding Drill:* Players 1 and 2 start at elbows of free-throw lane. Coach shoots and 1 and 2 go hard to the ball. They play the ball until someone scores or it goes out of bounds (diagram 2).

4) *Two-on-Two Rebounding:* Two coaches are at the guard positions. Players 1 and 2 must react defensively when the ball is passed guard to guard. When a coach shoots, players 1 and 2 must block out (diagram 3).

5) *Rebounding Outlet Continues Drill:* Player 1 passes to 2, 1 jab fakes and receives pass from 2. Player 1 throws ball to the right side of board and rebounds the ball and makes an outlet passto player 3. Player 3 passes to 4 and the drill continues. Player 1

Diagram 3

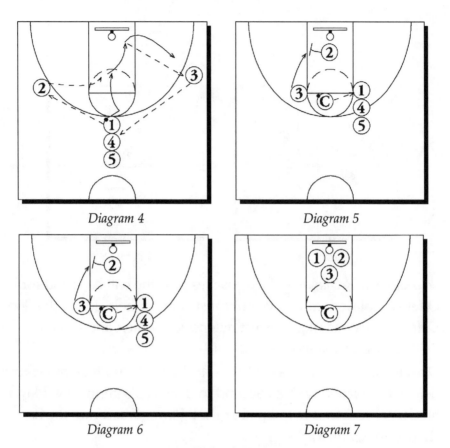

Diagram 4   Diagram 5

Diagram 6   Diagram 7

replaces 3, 3 goes to the end of the line (see diagram 4).

6) *Two-on-One Drill:* Coach stands at free-throw line and passes the ball to player 1 or 3. Player 2 must go opposite the pass and block. Shooter follows her shot and they play until 2 rebounds or 1 and 3 score (diagram 5).

7) *Toughness Drill:* Players must stay in the lane, and they cannot dribble. The coach starts the drill with a shot or a pass. Players try and keep each other from scoring. Player stays in until she scores three baskets. Players keep trying to put the ball in the basket even after made shots while the other two players are contesting her. If the ball flies way out of hte lane, let it go and the coach will enter another ball with a shot immediately (diagram 6).

8) *Three-on-Three Rebounding:* Two coaches pass the between them. The offensive players remain stationary and the defense must react on each pass. When the coach shoots, 1-2-3 must block (diagram 7).

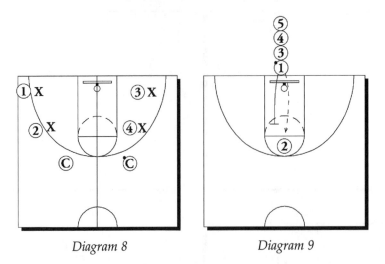

Diagram 8   Diagram 9

9) *Four-on-Four Rebounding*: Two coaches pass the ball back and forth. Offensive players can move but must stay on their side of the floor. Defense must maintain correct defensive position and block out when the ball is shot (diagram 8).

10) *One-on-One Close-out*: Player 1 rolls the ball to 2 and then moves into defensive position with a hand up to distract 2's jump shot. Player 1 blocks out as 2 tries to follow her shot. Player 1 becomes the next shooter (diagram 9).

11) *Three-on-Three Rebounding*: Have players slide across lane continuously. Coach will shoot the ball and player sliding will yell shot. Players sliding in the lane must go and block out player outside the lane and secure three defensive rebounds in a row. Have offense players crash the glass and each player in the lane must communicate and find a man outside the lane to box out. After three consecutive defensive rebounds, change the offense(diagrams 10 and 11).

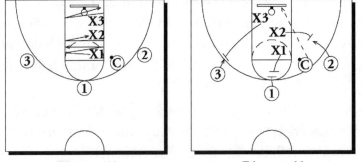

Diagram 10   Diagram 11

Coach Vanessa Blair
Mount St. Mary's College
Emmitsburg, Maryland

Four-in-the-Paint

Purpose:
To improve rebounding and transition defense.

Organization:
The team is divided into two units who compete against each other throughout the drill. The drill is generally run for eight or 10 minutes and the score is kept. One point is given for each defensive rebound, one point is given for a made shot, and two points are given for an offensive rebound.

1) Four defensive players (triangles) begin with at least one foot inside of the lane. Four offensive players (circles) begin on the perimeter. In addition, there is a defensive outlet player (triangle #1) and an offensive outlet player (circle #1). A coach is positioned underneath the basket with the ball.

Diagram 1

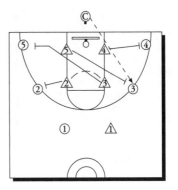

Diagram 2

2) The coach underneath the basket begins the drill by throwing the ball to one of the offensive players on the perimeter (offensive player 3 in the diagram) and at the same time will call out the name of one of the defensive players in the paint (defensive player 5 in the diagram). The offensive player who receives the ball takes a jump shot and follows her shot, while the defensive player whose name is called closes out on the player to whom the ball is thrown and boxes out the shooter.

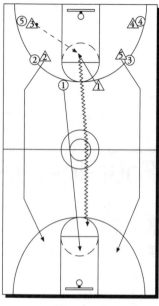

Diagram 3

3) The other defensive players must then locate and box out the remaining offensive players (this includes finding the player whom the called defender has left). The offensive players, except for the outlet, crash the boards for the offensive rebound. If the shot is made, the offense receives one point. If the shot is missed and an offensive player rebounds, the outlet player runs to the ball, calls for the pass and the offense receives two points. If the defense rebounds, they look to outlet the ball and run the floor in transition.

4) The five triangles will then break to the other end of the floor against the five circles. They will attempt to score in transition,

Diagram 4

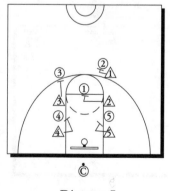

Diagram 5

secondary break, or set offense and will
play until the circles defensive rebound.
The triangles are given one point for the
defensive   rebound, one point if they
score offensively at the other end, and
two points for every offensive rebound
they might get at the other end.

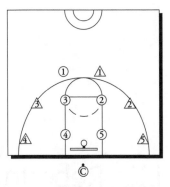

Diagram 6

The drill continues after either a score or a
defensive rebound. The players are reset in
their original positions at the other end of the floor and the coach
throws the ball to another offensive player on the perimeter for the
shot and calls out the name of another defender to close out and box
out. The drill continues in this manner until all four offensive players
on the perimeter have shot. After all perimeter players have shot, the
outlet player has a chance to shoot to complete the cycle for her unit.

Coach Stephanie V. Gaitley
Long Island University
Brooklyn, New York

LIU Rebounding Series

Purpose:

The objective of these drills is to teach the importance of rebounding, with an emphasis on boxing out.

Organization:

1) *5-on-5 Rotation Rebounding*: Five offensive players (O) line up inside the 3-point line. Five defensive players (X) match up with each offensive player. X's begin rotating as the coaches pass the ball. When a coach shoots the ball, X's must find O's to box out. The drill is not over until X makes an outlet pass to a coach. If offense gets the rebound they play it out. Each group goes for two minutes each on defense. Two points are given for a score and an offensive rebound (diagram 1).

Diagram 1

2) *Circle Box Out*: The ball is placed on the floor in the middle of the free-throw line. Defense (X's) must box out for five seconds, preventing O's from getting the ball (diagram 2).

Diagram 2

3) *Rough House: 1-on-1-on-1.* Anything goes in this drill. The coach takes the first shot and whoever rebounds tries to score. There are three dribbles maximum, and the players must score in the paint.

Diagram 3

Coach Stephanie V. Gaitley
Long Island University
Brooklyn, New York

1-on-1 Rebounding

Purpose:
The objective of this drill is to teach rebounding and desire for the ball.

Diagram 1

Organization:
Players start lined up at each elbow with the last player in each line as an outlet. A coach is positioned inside the circle near the free-throw line.

1) The coach begins the drill by shooting a basket. Two players (one from each line) are rebounding against each other. Whoever gets the rebound will turn to the outside and pass the ball to the outlet on the same side of the court. The player who rebounded then gets the ball back and plays one-on-one on the wing against the player who did not get the rebound.

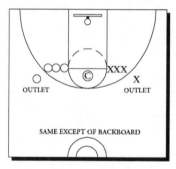

Diagram 2

2) Forwards are usually on one end of the court and the guards at another. Forwards will outlet, post up on the block, get it back and look to score.

Diagram 3

CHAPTER SEVEN

Post Player Drills

Coach Jack Miller
Rider University
Lawrenceville, New Jersey

Feeding the Post

Purpose:

To improve catching, reading the defense and shooting in the post.

Organization:

One passer is positioned at the right and left wing. Put four players under the basket.

1) Player 1 posts up big on the right low block showing where she wants the ball. Player C1 feeds player 1 with a pass, forcing her to go get the ball.

2) P1 catches the ball and brings it into her chin.

3) Next, P1 will look to the middle over her right shoulder to read the imaginary de fender.

4) After looking to the middle, P1 will make a post move going to the basket.

5) As P1 gets her own rebound, she outlets to C2 and reposts on the left low block.

6) P2 outlets to C1 and posts up on the right low block.

7) C1 and C2 pass into P1 and P2 forcing each to go get the ball.

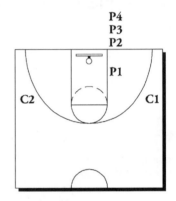

Diagram 1

Diagram 2

8) Both P1 and P2 must "chin" the ball and look middle to read the defense.

9) After reading the defense, P1 and P2 can make a post move to the basket.

10) P1 shoots and rebounds her ball, then goes to the end of the line. P2 rebounds and outlets to C2; P3 outlets to C1.

Coaching Points:

♦ Player will be able to show a target hand where she wants the ball.

♦ Player will be able to go after the ball and bring it into her body.

♦ Player will be able to look middle and read the defense.

♦ Player will be able to perform a post move (drop step, turn around jumper, baby hook, or an up-and-under move).

Coach Jessica Smith
Miami University of Ohio
Oxford, Ohio

Tap and Finish Drill

Purpose:
This drill is designed to strengthen both the left and right hand, rebounding and finishing skills. This drill can be used by both posts and guards.

Organization:
The player gets one ball and stands facing the backboard on the right side of the basket. The player's shoulders should be square to the backboard. To initiate the drill, begin to try one-handed taps off the backboard. If the player is having trouble with one-handed taps, try using both hands every other time. The player will tap the ball up to the backboard five times in a row. On the sixth, rip the ball down in a "Z" pattern, but make sure the player keeps the ball above her shoulders. This is done to secure the rebound and rip it down strong. She must then keep her inside elbow (on this side it will be her left elbow) up and pointed toward the center of the lane. The player will then jump and extend toward the rim and power the ball up against the backboard and through the hoop. She must use her right hand on the right side and left hand on the left side. She must not dribble! Then she will move to the other side of the rim and work on the left. The players will continue to move back and forth. As they get better, players should test themselves on how many they can do in a row without a miss or fumble.

Duffy Burns, Former Coach
Cleveland State University
Cleveland, Ohio

Post Moves

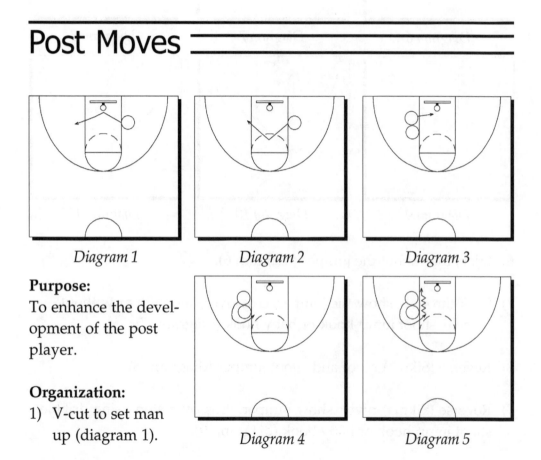

| Diagram 1 | Diagram 2 | Diagram 3 |

| Diagram 4 | Diagram 5 |

Purpose:
To enhance the development of the post player.

Organization:

1) V-cut to set man up (diagram 1).

2) Post up above the block (diagram 2).

3) Drop step, crab dribble, power move (diagram 3).

4) Step, shoot jumper (diagram 4).

5) Step through, show jumper, crossover step with or without dribble, shoot lay-up or power move (diagram 5).

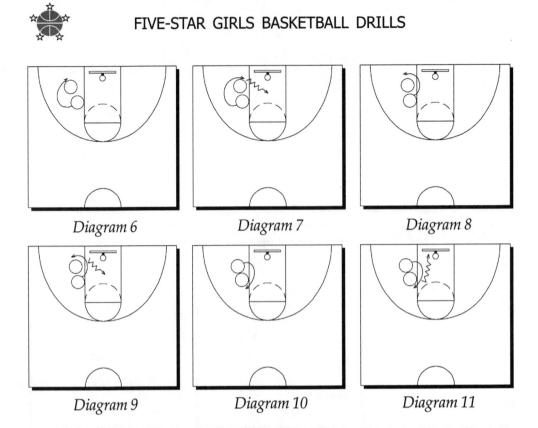

Diagram 6   Diagram 7   Diagram 8

Diagram 9   Diagram 10   Diagram 11

6) Stick, then shoot the jumper (diagram 6).

7) Stick through, show the jumper, crossover step with or without dribble, shoot jump hook or baby hook (diagram 7).

8) Reverse (Sikma) pivot and shoot jumper (diagram 8).

9) Reverse (Sikma) pivot, show jumper, crossover step using dribble, shoot jump hook or baby hook (diagram 9).

10) Reverse (Sikma) pivot and shoot jumper (diagram 10).

11) Reverse (Sikma) pivot, show jumper, crossover step using the dribble, shoot a lay-up or power move (diagram 11).

Coach Greg T. Collins
University of Louisville
Louisville, Kentucky

Two Balls-Two Post Players

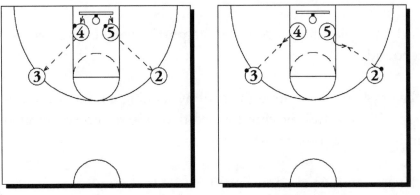

Diagram 1   Diagram 2

Purpose:
To improve catching, reading the defense and shooting in the post.

Organization:
Post players 4 and 5 each have a ball and face the backboard. Passers, players 2 and 3, are in position to receive an outlet and make an entry pass.

1) Players 4 and 5 toss the ball off the board, getting the rebound and making an outlet to the guard on their side (diagram 1).

2) As the perimeter players make an entry pass to the post, the post players exit the lane, catching the ball and landing with a two-footed "crow hop." This allows the post to execute a post move using either foot as the pivot foot (diagram 2).

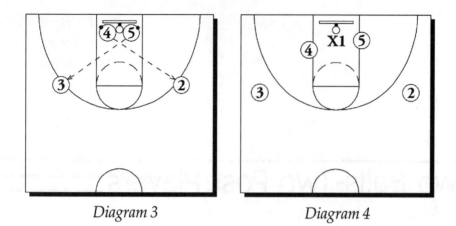

Diagram 3   Diagram 4

3) Each post player then completes a post move, getting her own rebound.

4) Players 4 and 5 continue the drill by making a pass out to the opposite side and moving toward that side to receive another pass and execute another post move (diagram 3).

5) Players continue at game speed for 1½ to 2 minutes.

Variation:
Add a single defender (diagram 4) to mix up guarding the post players.

Coaching Points:
♦ Post players work on game shots at game speed.
♦ Work on a variety of moves and countermoves.
♦ Perimeter players work.

Coach Greg T. Collins
University of Louisville
Louisville, Kentucky

Two Balls-Two Post Players-Fan Out

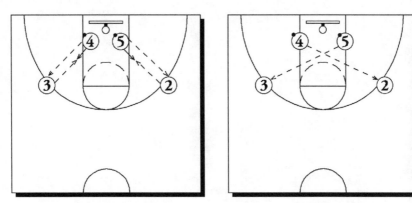

Diagram 1   *Diagram 2*

Purpose:
To improve post play.

Organization:
This drill is the same as "2 ball-2 posts" except the passing.

1) After players 4 and 5 have completed their post move, they make an outlet pass to the perimeter player on their side.

2) The perimeter player will make a return pass to the post (diagram 1).

3) After catching the pass with a two-footed jump shot (crow hop) out of the lane, the post player will fan the ball out to the opposite way (diagram 2).

225

4) Each post will make a cut to the ball to make another post scoring move (diagram 3).

5) Repeat the passing after getting their own rebound. Continue for one minute.

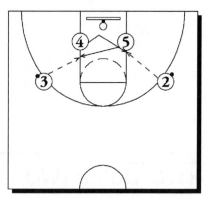

Diagram 3

Allison Greene, Former Coach
Old Dominion University
Norfolk, Virginia

Post Versatility

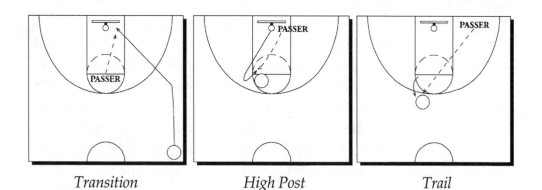

| Transition | High Post | Trail |

Purpose:

Post players are no longer limited to the blocks. In fact, to go to the next level, it is imperative that posts have a more versatile inside-out game. Scoring lay-ups in the paint cannot be the only place a post is effective. This drill implements four main scoring areas from where a post must be able to score. The four areas are:

♦ *Transition*
♦ *High Post*
♦ *Trail*
♦ *Block*

Organization:

The post player begins at half court on one side of the floor. The passer waits at the foul line with a ball. The player runs the lane and cuts in, at game speed, to the basket. She receives the ball on the run for a lay-up. The passer rebounds. After shooting, make or miss, the post goes immediately to the opposite elbow for a jumper. The passer

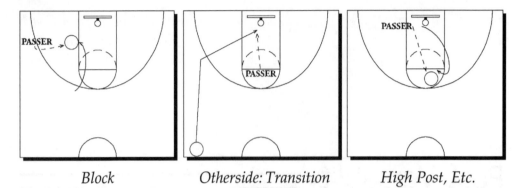

Block   *Otherside: Transition*   *High Post, Etc.*

again rebounds. The post then fades back to the top of the circle and takes a three point shot in the trail position. As the passer again rebounds, the post goes to the same side low block, receives a pass, and makes a strong power move. All this time the passer is both rebounding and passing to her partner. Once the post has taken the shot on the blocks, she sprints back to half court and runs in again for a transition lay-up. Then, back to the high post. Then, the trail. Lastly, the low block again. She repeats this series until she makes a total of 10 shots. The made shots can be at any or all of the spots. Once she has made 10, she sprints to the other side of the half court and runs the lane for a lay-up. She then proceeds to the opposite elbow for the same sequence at the other side. After she has made 10 total shots, have her go to the free-throw line. Repeat.

Coach Greg T. Collins
University of Louisville
Louisville, Kentucky

Get Open: Post-up, Step, Spin and Pin⌐

Purpose:
To improve post play.

Organization:
The offensive post player standing
facing the lane will usually find herself
facing the defender also. The coach or
player has the ball on the wing,
freethrow line extended (diagram 1).

Diagram 1

1) The offensive post player steps with her top foot, placing it directly
   between the defender's feet (the step).

2) Next, the player will make an aggressive reverse pivot on the foot
   that was placed between the
   defender's feet (the spin).

3) The post player pins the defender by
   becoming a wide target, always
   keeping her hands open to the ball,
   her elbows out away from her body
   and showing her numbers to the
   passer.

Diagram 2

4) As the defender attempts to get around, the offensive post player maintains contact with the defender and continues to present a wide target to the passer, always showing her numbers directly to the ball (diagram 2).

5) Catch the entry pass, "chin it" and pass it back. Continue for 20 to 30 seconds.

Coach Greg T. Collins
University of Louisville
Louisville, Kentucky

High-Post Scoring Series

Purpose:
To improve post play.

Organization:
Post players create two lines beginning outside the lane just below the block.

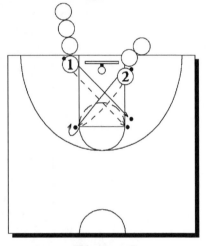

Diagram 1

1) The first player does a self-toss, tossing the ball up so that it bounces around the elbow area of the lane. She follows her toss, catching it after the first bounce. She should jump stop around the elbow area, make a forward pivot and shoot a jump shot. After the first player has gone through the middle of the lane, the player in the opposite line makes the same self-toss.

2) Each player follows her shot for the rebound or gets the ball out of the net and goes to the next line.

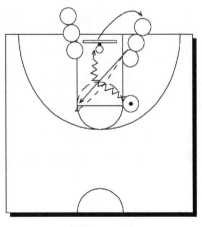

Diagram 2

3) The series:

♦ Jump shot (diagram 1)

231

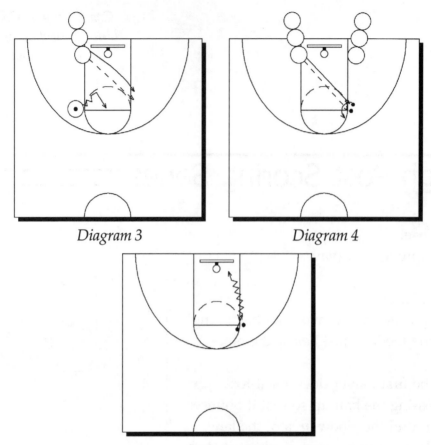

Diagram 3   *Diagram 4*

Diagram 5

- ◆ Swing through and drive, one dribble (diagram 2)
- ◆ Swing through and drive, step-back jumper (diagram 3)

Variation:
- ◆ Players can make reverse pivot after their jump stop and work on driving straight down the lane (diagram 4).

- ◆ Reverse pivot and jump shot.

- ◆ Shot fake and drive, using a crossover step (diagram 5).

Coach Joe Ciampi
Auburn University
Auburn, Alabama

Post Bank Shots

Purpose:
To improve shooting in the low post.

Organization:
You need two chairs and two balls to
run this drill. Place chairs one step away
from the lane and between the block
and first hash mark. Each player has one
minute to shoot 12 shots. Players start at
chair one with their back to the basket.

Diagram 1

Player picks up the ball from the chair and pivots to the baseline and
shoots a bank shot. The player rebounds her own shot and places the
ball back in chair one. Player sprints to chair two and repeats action.
Record the number of shots made.

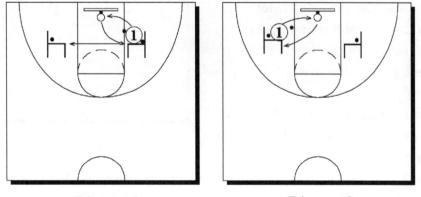

Diagram 2   *Diagram 3*

Coach Roberto Thompson
Catalina Magnet High School
Tucson, Arizona

Post Fast Break to Secondary

Purpose:
To improve shooting in the low post.

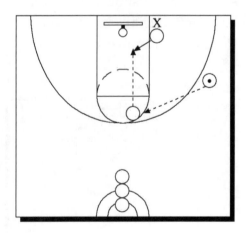

Diagram 1

Organization:
1) The post players line up in the middle of the court, with basketballs. The coach is on one side. The post player passes to coach on the right wing. The post runs straight down the middle to a post defender under the basket. The offensive post players her right foot in the middle of post defender's legs, then receives the pass from the coach and scores. The post defender goes to the end of the line, post player becomes the post defender, and the next player goes.

Diagram 2

2) Next phase begins in the same way as above, but the next post player in line runs to the high post. The low post is covered by a three-quarter low front. The coach then passes to the high post. The low post offensive player

steps over the defender, staying low and wide with her hands up, seals and catches the pass from the high post and scores. The post defender becomes the offensive player, the low post player becomes the defender, the high post player goes to the low post, and the drill begins again.

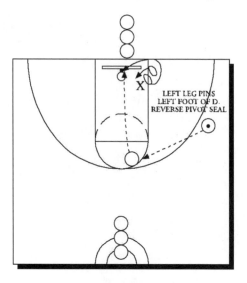

Diagram 3

3) The final phase begins the same way as above. The low post is covered by a three-quarter high front that cannot be stepped over, over the top. The low post steps back with their left foot behind the defender's left leg, reverse-pivots and seals, puts the left bar arm up and puts under the armpit of the defender to create a passing angle. Right arm goes up to give a target. The high post must bounce pass to the low post, because a direct pass can be knocked away. The post player catches and score and rotates as in the previous phase.

CHAPTER EIGHT
Defensive Drills

Coach Cindy Griffin
St. Joseph's University
Philadelphia, Pennsylvania

3-on-4 Half Court Defensive Drill

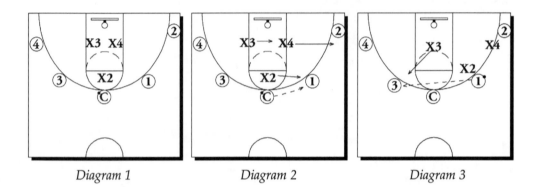

| *Diagram 1* | *Diagram 2* | *Diagram 3* |

Purpose: To improve stance, lateral movement, closeout technique and communication.

Organization:

1) The coach has the ball up top. She can pass to any of the four offensive players along the three-point line. The defensive players have to move on the pass and talk about who they have (diagram 1).

2) If the coach passes to O1, then X2 is closer to the ball, so she stops the ball. X4 will deny O2 and X3 will help in the middle lane (diagram 2).

3) If O1 passes to O2, X4 has O2 covered (diagram 3).

4) If O1 passes to O3, then X3 would have to get out to her.

5) X4 and X2 have to talk. If X4 takes O4, then X2 gets back to the middle of lane.

Cheryl Reeve, Assistant Coach
WNBA Charlotte Sting
Charlotte, North Carolina

4-on-4 Ball Side/Help Side

Purpose:
The focus of this drill is on the basic fundamentals of man-to-man defense: ball side and help side. Points of emphasis for the drill are positioning relative to the ball, determination of the "box" rule, movement on the flight of the ball, communication and active hands.

Diagram 1

Organization:
Have four players take offensive positions at the top of the key area about 15 feet apart and at the low wing areas on each side of the floor. Assign defenders to each offensive player. Draw either an imaginary line down the middle of the lane (which would split the court into two sides, "boxes" if you will) OR lay tape down to illustrate the point of two "boxes." This would be a good idea, especially early in the season when trying to establish the basics. The fundamental box rule establishes that if the ball is in a box, then defensive players guarding players in the box should be in a denial position. If the ball is not in a box, then all defensive players in that box are in help position. Simply stated: If the ball

Diagram 2

Diagram 3

239

Diagram 3

is in your box, DENY; if the ball is not in your box, HELP.

The player who is guarding the ball declares "ball" and takes on the ball defensive position. On-the-ball defense points of emphasis would include the verbal call of "ball," footwork forcing the offensive player to the desired area of the floor, and active hands ready to deflect any passes. The "on-the-ball" defender's goal is to control the offensive player's movements through active hands and active feet.

The defensive players not guarding the ball must determine whether that ball is in their box or not. If so, the defensive player takes a denial position on her player; if not, then she declares "help side" and should take position relative to the location of the ball first and then the player she is guarding. "Help-side" positioning would include an active stance that would enable seeing both the ball and the player being guarded by that player.

The four offensive players pass the ball on the coach's command. The coach should be looking for proper positioning of each player. Additionally, the coach must demand movement *on the flight* of the ball from one player to the next, as opposed to the defense shifting after the offense receives the ball. This is crucial to maintaining good defensive positioning.

Note: Many defensive principles can be added to this drill once the basics are established (for example, defending screens, taking charges, blocking out, etc.).

Coach Jody Conradt
University of Texas
Austin, Texas

Closeout Technique Drill

Purpose:
To improve closing-out skills

Organization:
  When the coach slaps the ball, each
player pushes hard toward the coach in
a closeout position at the free-throw
line. When the coach throws the pass to
a manager, each person must jump to
the ball in a deny position. The next line
of players will repeat the same drill.

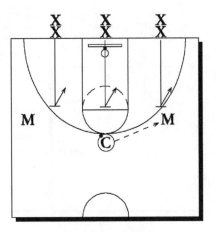

Coaching Points:

♦ Knees are bent.

♦ Hands must be below waist on the approach.

♦ Inside foot is up with the outside ankle to the corner.

Coach A.C. McCullers
Clayton College & State University
Morrow, Georgia

Defensive Progression

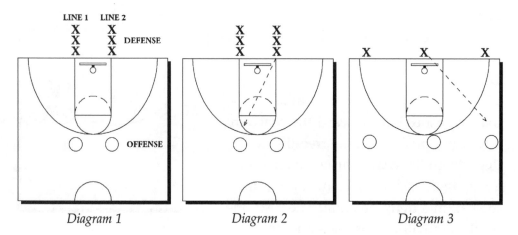

| Diagram 1 | Diagram 2 | Diagram 3 |

Purpose:

To improve one-on-one defensive concepts.

Organization:

1) The players line up for 1-on-1 defense in two lines. The defense must roll ball to her elbow. Players in line one go first. The defensive player should close out offensive player. Retreat step on first move. Box out on shot. As a variation, the coach can limit the offensive player to a set number of dribbles (diagram 1).

2) Progress to 2-on-2. The players cross pass (or roll) ball to start. The emphasis is on close out. The players play screen-and-roll (hedge screens). Be sure the players cut the cutter and deny flash. Players should also watch "ball-you-man" spacing (one pass away) (diagram 2).

3) Progress to 3-on-3. The stresses are the same as 2-on-2. Add help and recover and rotation on baseline drives. Work on post defense (diagrams 3 and 4).

4) Progress to 4-on-4 shell. Work on all defensive principles
   (diagram 5):
   a) close out
   b) retreat steps
   c) help & recover
   d) cut the cutter
   e) hedge on screens
   f) deny the flash
   g) box out on screens
   h) rotate on drive

Coach should stress offensive moves and techniques!

5) Progress to 5-on-5. Run full offense vs. defense. Stress help on lobs
   to the post. Taking off changes (diagrams 6, 7 and 8).

Coaching Tip:
Position post at different postions.

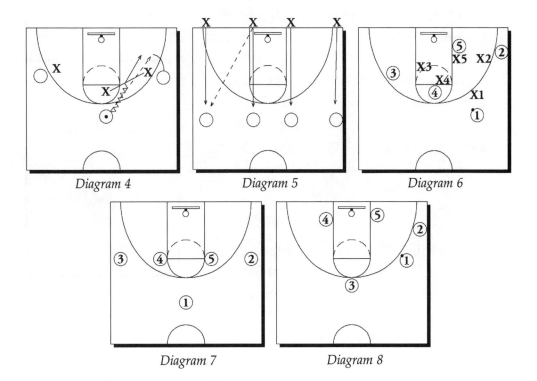

Diagram 4   Diagram 5   Diagram 6

Diagram 7   Diagram 8

Coach Jill M. Pizzotti
Saint Louis University
St. Louis, Missouri

Defensive Slide/Dive Drill

Purpose:
To teach proper first-step footwork on defense.

Organization:

1) Player A is in a defensive stance. The coach rolls a ball to the block. Player A slides to the block (with outside foot), picks the ball up and throws a chest pass back to the coach. The coach has already rolled the second ball to the other block (diagram 1).

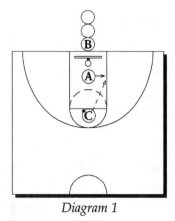

Diagram 1

2) Player A slides block to block passing balls back to the coach. After 15-20 seconds, the coach rolls a ball toward the sideline. Player A sprints, dives to save the ball and passes it up to B, who has sprinted toward A calling for the ball (diagram 2).

Diagram 2

3) During this drill, the second player in line (B), must call left or right, which helps player A know which foot to step with toward the block. Players have a tendency to bring their feet together before taking the first step.

Coach Jody Conradt
University of Texas
Austin, Texas

Full Court Zig-Zag

Purpose:
To improve full-court pressure

Organization:
   The offense goes side to side, bringing the ball up the court. Early-on, offense goes ¾ speed. Defense works on technique.

Variation: Offense dribbles two balls.

Coaching Points:

♦ Defense plays nose on the ball and backside to opposite baseline

♦ Slide down, don't run.

♦ No hands early — defense should wait for offense to give it to them.

♦ Don't take it — cut the drive off, but don't chest.

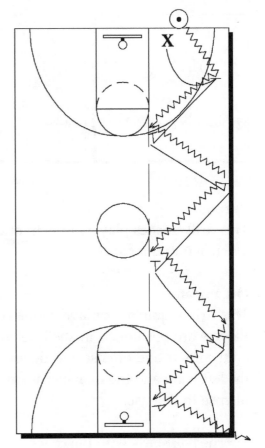

Coach Kay Yow
North Carolina State University
Raleigh, North Carolina

Help and Recover to 3-on-3 Live

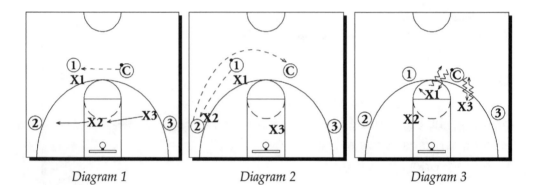

Diagram 1	*Diagram 2*	*Diagram 3*

Purpose:
This drill teaches players to help and recover. It also teaches proper defensive rotations.

Organization:
This drill requires six players, one coach, two balls and one manager. Players are positioned in shell defense spots (offense and defense in both corners and offense and defense on right wing). The coach is on the left wing and the manager is under the basket. Players rotate from offense to defense.

1) The ball starts with the coach, who passes to player 1. On the pass, defensive players adjust (diagram 1).

2) Player 1 passes to 2. Again, defensive players adjust (diagram 2).

3) The ball is skip-passed back to the coach. The coach drives right requiring X1 to help stop penetration. The coach then drives left

requiring X3 to help stop penetration (diagram 3).

4) The coach passes to player 3, who
   penetrates the baseline. For the
   sake of the drill, X3 allows 3 to beat
   her (diagram 4).

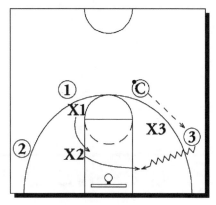

Diagram 4

5) On the penetration, X2 slides over
   to help and X1 drops.

6) Player 3 tries to pass across baseline
   to 2. X1 knocks the ball out-of-
   bounds to the manager, and the coach throws a "live" ball to 1.

7) Play is live (3-on-3).

Coaching Points:

♦ Good communication between players.

♦ Give early help and recover quickly.

♦ Players helping must have good body position in order to prevent
  the coach from getting to the basket. If the player's body position is
  too open, the coach will have a direct path to the basket.

♦ Help on the baseline should occur outside the lane line, otherwise
  it has arrived too late.

♦ The ball needs to move quickly. This hould be a very fast-paced,
  intense drill.

Variation:
Trap the ball handler on the baseline.

Coach David Glass
Virginia Commonwealth University
Richmond, Virginia

Progressive Defensive Drills ═══

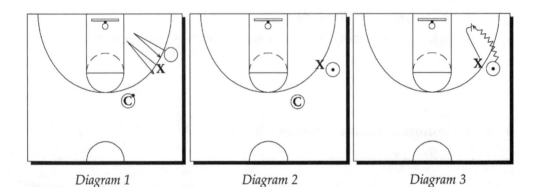

| Diagram 1 | Diagram 2 | Diagram 3 |

Purpose:
To develop players' defensive strategy and man-to-man concepts, step-by-step.

Organization:
This is a progressive defensive drill that covers (1) wing deny, (2) defense on the ball, (3) guarding the dribble, (4) reacting to a pass that has been made, (5) help-and-recover technique, (6) live one-on-one defense, and (7) blocking out and rebounding. This is an excellent drill because it helps to develop many good defensive habits and is a good defensive conditioning drill. In this drill you must work very hard at the defensive end of the court for several minutes.

1) *Wing Deny*: The drill starts with a defender guarding an offensive player on the wing. A passer attempts to complete a pass to the offensive player who must move to get open on the wing. We teach the defensive player to be in a position up the passing line ap-

proximately three feet off the offensive player. The defense must successfully prevent the offensive player
from receiving the ball for a count of
five seconds, one time (diagram 1).

Diagram 4

2) *On-the-Ball Stance*: Now do this drill
again; however, if the pass can be
made to the offensive player, do so
and stop! Check the defensive stance
and the position of the feet. Do not
allow middle penetration and so we
want to see that the defensive player
is positioned to force the ball to the
baseline (diagram 2).

Diagram 5

3) *Guarding the Dribble*: The drill begins
again with the wing deny and if the
pass can be made then we pass the
ball. Do not stop the drill when the
offensive player catches the ball,
rather allow her to take two hard dribbles and then she must pick
up the ball. Once the defense stops the ball, the defense gets tight
to the offensive player, chest-to-chest, and crosses her hands and
mirrors the ball. If the offense was able to penetrate to the middle
of the floor, then the defensive player must do three push-ups.
Remember, do not allow middle penetration, so if this happens in
any drill during practice, the player will automatically do three
push-ups. Teach them to call out,"dead, dead, dead" to let the
other defensive players know that the offensive player has used the
dribble option and to deny all passes (diagram 3).

4) *Jumping to the Ball*: Get players in the habit of moving in the direction of the ball as a pass is made. This is called "jumping to the
ball." Start the drill all over again and get to the dead-ball situation, then have the offensive player make a pass back out to the

coach. Now the defensive player must jump to the ball. The offensive player will attempt to make a face cut, that is to cut between the ball and the defensive player. Always maintain a ball-you-man relationship on defense and never allow the player being guarded to cut between the player and the ball. As the offensive player starts to make a face cut, the defensive player will be in a position to bump the cutter and not allow the face cut to happen. Stop the drill after the defender bumps the cutter and gets back into a good stance to deny the pass back to the offensive player on the wing (diagram 4).

5) *Help and Recover*: This a progressive drill, so start over. The defensive player now must deny the pass to the wing, get in to a good on-the-ball defensive stance if the ball is caught on the wing, force the ball toward the baseline and force a dead-ball situation, jump to the ball on a pass and maintain a ball-you-man relationship, bump any attempted face cut and return to a good wing-deny defensive stance. At this point, during the wing deny, the coach will start to make a ball-side drive to the basket. Defender should now see the drive and make a move to help defense by stopping the ball. When the defender forces the coach to stop the dribble move and pass the ball back out to the offensive player on the wing, the defender must recover back to the ball, under control, by using a closeout step. This a "help-and-recover" move. At this point, this becomes a live one-on-one drill. Once a shot is taken, the defense must block out and sprint to recover the rebound (diagram 5).

This is a great drill to use throughout the year. Use it in preseason to teach defensive technique and use it during the season to reinforce good defensive habits. Encourage players to work very hard in this drill and to be very vocal. Have each of them to do it correctly one time. This drill is more competitive than spending five or 10 minutes of station work doing a wing-deny drill. This is also a drill that players can do in the off-season to improve their defensive skills.

1-on-1 Wing Drill

Purpose:
To improve 1-on-1 defense.

Organization:
The offensive player cuts to the wing. Receiving the pass from the coach, the player goes to a 1-on-1 situation (2 dribbles max).

Coaching Points:

♦ Deny entry.

♦ Force the player to the corner.

♦ Make offense catch as far out as possible.

♦ React straight back on jab step; approach top foot-back foot.

Coach Kevin Chaney
Solono Community College
Fairfield, California

Rip Throughs Defensive Drill

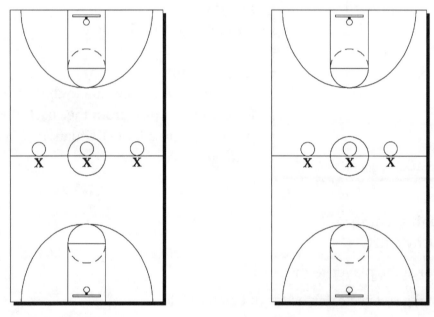

Diagram 1   Diagram 2

Purpose:
To develop quicker change of direction on the rip-through. To contain penetration and reduce chances of being beaten off the dribble. It also helps develop lateral change-of-direction movement.

Organization:
Offense can rip through and jab from the triple-threat position only. The defense must quickly shift to the ball trying to keep their heads on the ball. Go 10 seconds and then rotate. You can rip through on the whistle or let the players play independently.

Coach Kristy Curry
Purdue University
West Lafayette, Indiana

Triangle Defensive Drill

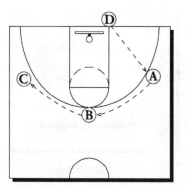

Purpose:
To teach defensive positioning.

Organization:
Player D passes to player A and closes out on A. Player D then gets in defensive position. Player A tries to drive by and score; if she can't, then player A passes to B. Defense jumps to the ball and denies A. Player B passes to C. Player D opens and sprints to midline. Then player D denies A's flash cut.

Coach Kevin Chaney
Solono Community College
Fairfield, California

Help for the Lob/the Skip

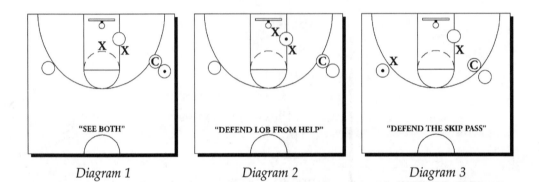

| Diagram 1 | Diagram 2 | Diagram 3 |

Purpose:

To improve peripheral vision from the help position and improve the reaction to the pass. Must move quickly while the ball is in the air.

Organization:

Divide players into teams of three. Player 1 delivers the lob, player 2 is the weakside shooter or penetrator, and player 3 is the help defender. To work on lob, don't use help defense. Player 3 passes to lob or skip. Defender must defend the lob or steal the skip or be there when it's caught. After a steal, rotate a new 3 on to the court. When it's their turn again, they'll play different spots. Repeat until all have gone and played all spots. Let the players communicate who will play where. This teaches them to talk before their turn. When the whistle blows they sprint to their new positions.

Coach John Ishee
Life University
Marietta, Georgia

X-Out Drill

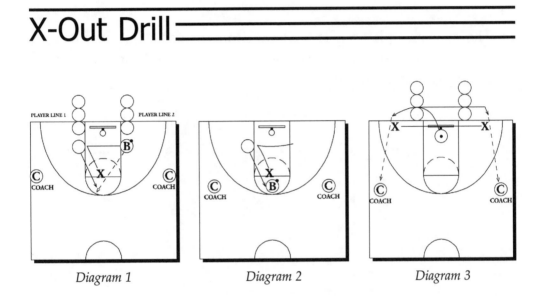

| Diagram 1 | Diagram 2 | Diagram 3 |

Purpose:
To develop 1-on-1 offense and defense. Improve outlet passing.

Organization:
1) This drill starts with two single-file lines at and behind the baseline (diagram 1).

2) The player with the basketball (B) rolls the ball to the top of the key. She then touches the opposite black before closing out to defend the player that vacated there (player line #1). Block to retrieve the basketball at the top of the key.

3) The player in line 1 must square up in a triple-threat position before trying to shoot or drive.

4) The offensive player with the basketball keeps possession as long as she comes up with the ball, whether that's from an offensive

rebound or from beating her opponent 1-on-1 to the basketball (diagram 2).

5) Once the defensive player gets possession of the ball, she makes an outlet pass to the coaches stationed above the three-point arch. If possession changes due to a made basket, then the defense becomes the offense. Offense then goes to play defense.

6) The defensive player gets the ball, clears the basket and the lane area. The offensive layer becomes the defender and pressures the outlet pass (diagram 3).

Group Defensive Drills

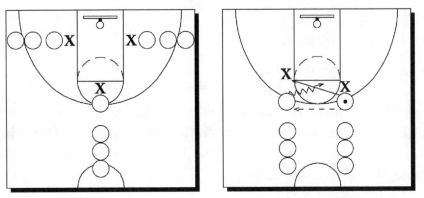

Diagram 1   Diagram 2

Purpose:
To improve overall defensive skills.

Organization:
1) *One-on-One:* This drill can be played from any spot on the floor, the three most common places are shown in diagram 1. Start ball within shooting distance and defender close. Defenders can either play with towel around their necks or with hands held behind their backs.

   The offensive player works on her footwork as well as the defensive player. Each offensive player executes each of the following plays:

   ◆ Fake shot and drive

   ◆ Fake shot, fake drive, shoot

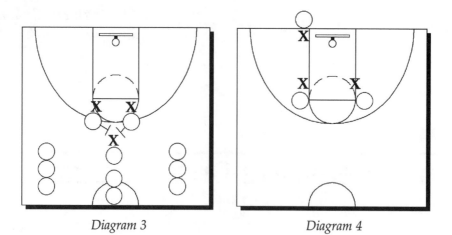

Diagram 3   Diagram 4

- ♦ Rocker step and go
- ♦ Crossover step and go

2) *Two-on-Two:* The offensive player passes to her partner, sets a pick and rolls to basket. Defense works on jump switches. The drill should also be practiced with guard-forward starting setup (diagram 2).

3) *Three-on-Three, Half Court (can also be started at the endline):* Middle player has ball and dribbles. The drill begins with a double high pick-and- roll and continues with three-on-three. Drill's emphasis is on jump switching and checking out on defensive rebounding (diagram 3).

Variation:
Begin with all three wide and pass and from middle player who then either picks for the player she passes to or picks away.

4) *Three-on-Three, Full Court:* Full-court 3-on-3 drill starting with ball out-of-bounds. First pass may not be past free-throw line extended and defense may two-time the receivers (diagram 4).

5) *Three-on-Two, Two-on-One Drill:* Begins with squad in three lines at the end of the court and two players at the other end waiting to defend. Play begins as a normal 3-on-2 fast-break drill. However,

when two defenders get the ball at the far end, they come back on attack against the original middle man on a 3-on-2 break.

Variation:
Set time clock at four minutes and make squad get 25 baskets in the time.

6) *Continuous Three-on-Two Drill:* Starts with two players at each end of the floor on defense. The first pass is from the coach to front player in line (1). Players C and D go down the court with player 1 in 3-on-2 working against A and B. If they score against A and B, defenders take ball out and

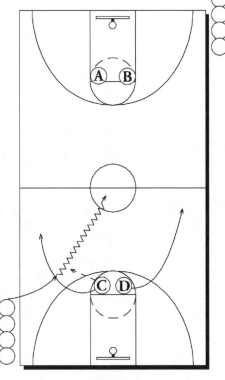

Diagram 5

pass to first player in other line (2) and join her on break. Defenders are next two players in line at far end. If there is no score, players rebound, clear and release to break. After players A and B leave the court, the next two players in line 2 take their place on defense (diagram 5).

Variation:
Set clock at 4:30. Squad must score 25 baskets (kept on board) before horn goes off. Laps for failure and drills run until they are successful.

Coach Greg T. Collins
University of Louisville
Louisville, Kentucky

Stop, Charge and Contest ══

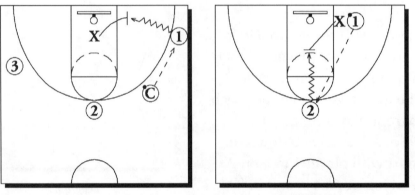

Diagram 1   *Diagram 2*

Purpose:
The objective of this drill is to teach post players how to be effective help-defenders.

Organization:
Three players start outside the three-point line and the post player is in the lane directly in front of the basket.

1) The coach begins the drill by passing to player 1. She immediately drives hard to the basket as if she beat her defender on the baseline side. The post defender must stop the ball outside the lane (diagram 1).

2) As soon as O1 is stopped, she passes to O2 at the top of the key. Player 2 drives straight to the basket. The post defender recovers

into a defensive position in front of
the ball and takes a charge (diagram
2).

3) As player 2 charges and the defender
takes the charge, player 2 passes out
to player 3 outside the three-point
line. The defender's challenge is to
get off the floor and contest the
three-point shooter (diagram 3).

Diagram 3

Player 3 goes to player 2's position
after completing the action, player 2
goes to player 1's position, and player 1 goes to the end of the line
or becomes the next defender. The post defender becomes player 3
on offense.

Coaching Points:

♦ When taking a charge, players must not put their hands down
to brace the fall. They might injure their wrists.

♦ Teach players to contest shots or to attempt to block shots in
such a way that they can still blockout for rebounding position.

Coach Kay Yow
North Carolina State University
Raleigh, North Carolina

Two Ball Closeout Drill

Purpose:
Teach players to contest jump shots while defending penetration by using solid man-to-man principles and positioning.

Organization:
There are two live players, one offensive player and one defensive player matched up on the left wing. One player is standing at the top of the key with a ball, and a coach is at the top of the key with a ball. A passer is on the right wing and in the right corner. You will also need a manager in the corner with a second ball. It is very important that all passers "zip" the ball to the next person. This drill should be very intense and taxing on the live defender. The drill should move very quickly.

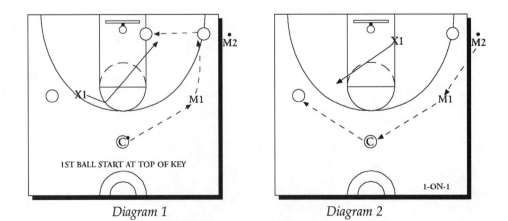

Diagram 1   Diagram 2

1) Player X1 gets proper defensive position as the ball is moved around the horn to the corner.

2) Player X1 must sprint to knock away the pass from the corner to the post.

3) As the ball is knocked, manager 2 passes the ball to manager 1 who fires the ball to the coach at the top of the key. The coach then throws to live offensive player on the left wing. The ball is moved around the key very quickly forcing X1 to spring from the block back out to her defensive assignment.

4) X1 must sprint and closeout as she nears the offensive person. X1 and O1 now play one-on-one live. Defender's goal is to get close enough to contest the jump shot and contain penetration. The drill is not over until the defender secures a rebound.

Coaching Points:
♦ Teach proper body position and angles.

♦ Stress the fundamentals of proper man-to-man defense.

♦ Teach players to breakdown (take "choppy" steps) as they near the offensive player.

♦ Stress the importance of staying low and being ready to push off laterally to contain penetration.

♦ Never allow penetration to the middle.

CHAPTER NINE

Basketball Miscellanea

Coach Matt Masiero
Five-Star Basketball Camp
Yonkers, New York

Setting Good Habits

20 SMALL DETAILS THAT MAKE A BIG DIFFERENCE

MAXIM: IF YOU DO IT IN PRACTICE, YOU'LL DO IT IN THE GAME!

The following practice guidelines were designed by me in July of 1997, while I was teaching the Team Defense Station at the Five-Star Boys' Basketball Camp, Pitt. IV session. It was during my instruction of the 'Shell Defense' that I began to notice most campers were demonstrating small, poor practice habits that had long frustrated me as a coach. It also reminded me of the numerous players that I have coached throughout the years that revealed the same idiosyncrasies. To relieve this frustration, I decided to create this list.

In the list of 20 details, I first point out the problem (turnover), then submit a recommendation (steal) and finally an example of what I mean. You will notice I make no reference to concrete fundamental skills such as passing/catching techniques (target zone), dribbling techniques (dribble w/head up) and/or shooting techniques (being balanced). I have purposely steered away from addressing such aspects of the game because I believe numerous coaches before me have done a tremendous job of rectifying those problem through various drills. I do however, address aspects of practicing passing/catching, dribbling and shooting such as when, where, how and what type that I believe are beneficial and critical to improve both the team and individual.

As a player/coach you may observe none, some or all of these practice habits in yourself or players, but at least this list will hopefully give you a reference to reflect upon. Another reason I developed this list is to help both players and teams improve through discipline, hard work and responsibility. If it helps one player/team to improve their overall practice habits then I will be happy, but if it helps them develop such life skills as good decision making and problem solving, discipline, hard work, communication, organization and responsibility, then the list has truly served its purpose.

Remember what Coach John Wooden once said: "I am a teacher of life first, then a coach, whatever that is." This philosophy is something we as coaches should all adopt, and I believe this list can help us become teachers of life by developing our players' critical and creative thinking skills through basketball.

Before you review the list, as an introduction I would like to give you an example of what the list is truly trying to accomplish. This example is one of a critical and creative thinking nature and has been implemented into my coaching practice.

♦ **Turnover**.*Limited Critical & Creative Thinking Skills:* Players often go along and do the norm.

♦ **Steal**. *Expanded Critical & Creative Thinking Skills:* Players need to enhance their critical and creative thinking skills during practice, by evaluating, assessing and analyzing every aspect of the game that requires them to solve problems and make decisions.

♦ **Example**: When any practice drill begins, rather than question a coach's authority, merely inquire about his or her philosophy and style/structure, so you can appreciate that point of view. My philosophy emphasizes the development of attitudes and dispositions that can be transferred into other situations. For example, players should try to transfer all possible knowledge/skills learned on the basketball court such as: discipline, hard work, responsibility, organization and communication to other contexts such as the classroom or job. Players should put as much effort and hard work into submitting a successful English term paper or becoming the best manager possible as they would improving their jump shot.

1 **Turnover.** *Lack of Hustle:* At the start of each drill, inbetween drills and during breaks.

Steal. *Hustling:* Time is crucial! Although it may seem so, practice doesn't last that long and time should not be wasted. Get there and get to work!

Example: During practice there are too many aspects to cover and time cannot be wasted in between or on one drill.

2 **Turnover.** *Nongame Condition Pre- & Post-Practice:* Certain shots taken or dribbling around during pre-practice, between drills and/or after practice that waste time and do not improve your game. Not working on your weaknesses.

Steal. *Game Condition Pre- & Post-Practice:* Again, time is crucial, so make use of pre- and post-practice time to improve your shooting and dribbling from different areas of the floor. In between drills put the ball down and get to the next drill. Work on your weaknesses.

Example: Taking half-court shots or dribbling between the legs in one area is not a game-like condition; focus the time to work on the weak areas of shooting and game conditioning dribbling.

3 **Turnover.** *Wasted Drills Offensive & Defensive:* Because the drill is either offensive or defensive in nature, the offense and/or defense tends to go through the motions, especially when it is a 5-0 drill.

Steal. *Productive Offensive & Defensive Practice:* This is extra time and the perfect opportunity to work on both the offensive/ defensive ends of the floor. Make the offense/defense work harder and improve.

Example: Develop the disposition of creativity and visualization. Practice the team's offensive and defensive philosophy when involved in drills of the opposite intent. When going 5-0 practice hard and pretend the offense or defense is present.

4   **Turnover.** *Blending Skills in Drills:* Only working on one skill for that specific drill.

Steal. *Many Skills In All Drills:* There are various skills that can be worked on and preexist in the drills, they just need more practice.

Example: Develop the attitude and disposition of flexibility. When a drill is primarily designed to improve shooting, remember that chances are a rebound must be taken down and a pass must be made in order for the next player to shoot. Work on all three phases of the game.

5   **Turnover.** *Lack of Attention/Focus:* Not listening or focusing on what is being taught during drills or when reviewing an opponent's scouting report.

Steal. *Familiarity with All Positions:* Learn all positions on the floor, all aspects of the drill and the opponent's tendencies.

Example: Keep eye contact on the coach and what is happening during drills at all times. Make sure to be familiar with what your opponent is going to do. If possible, sub in for teammates of a different position.

6   **Turnover.** *Talking and Listening:* There is a time to ask questions and a time to be quiet and listen.

Steal. *Timing:* During the explanation of drills strategically pick the opportune time to ask questions.

Example: Do not talk while on the sideline/baseline during a drill. Develop an open mind to what the coach is saying even though you may not initially agree. Once the coach is finished explaining, then ask questions.

7   **Turnover.** *Passing and Catching:* Making a poor pass a good catch.

Steal. *Catching and Passing:* Step to receive all passes and catch them all 2-handed by moving the body in position. Make crisp 1- and 2-handed passes with your outside hand and away from the defense.

Example: Do not try to catch passes 1-handed by trying to slap the ball. Do not stand still waiting to receive a pass. Remember, a steal or pickoff is catching someone's bad pass. Lastly, do not always pass 2-handed and across the body where the defender could be.

8 **Turnover.** *Lack of Concentration Shots:* Missing open shots close to the basket when there is no defender.

Steal. *Concentration Shots:* Focus on making the easy, open shots in all drills, especially with no defenders.

Example: When involved in drills such as the 5-man weave, focus on finishing lay-ups.

9 **Turnover.** *Making Excuses and Being a Spectator:* Taking the easy way out of responsibility and watching the game take place.

Steal. *Being Responsible and a Participant:* "Don't tell me the sea is rough, just bring the ship in." Don't think someone else will do it. Be the one who steps up and initiates the action.

Example: When coach needs a player for any drill, be the one who steps up and initiates the drill.

10 **Turnover.** *No I In Team:* Supposedly there is no (I) individual within the team.

Steal. *I Within Team:* True, that no individual is greater than the team, but the sum of each individual player can be greater than the team as a whole.

Example: If each individual is accountable, takes the responsibility of developing his or her game and makes a contribution, then the team will be much stronger, as opposed to letting teammates do the job.

11 **Turnover.** *Logical/Predictable Passing and Catching:* Players tend to throw passes that are logical and predictable. They also tend to catch passes facing the direction the ball came from.

Steal. *Illogical/Unpredictable Passing and Catching:* Make passes that the defense can't anticipate. Pass away from the next area anticipated. Catch the ball and be facing the basket so the defense doesn't know what the next move is.

Example: When the ball is passed from the wing most players have a tendency to catch looking at the passer. They should catch facing the basket in triple-threat (basketball) position. This forces the defense to have to defend three possibilities as opposed to one.

12 **Turnover.** *Non-Basketball Positioning:* Players always stand flat-footed and straight up.

Steal. *Basketball Positioning:* Be bent down and always on the balls of the feet. Be on the move.

Example: When defending, shooting, passing, catching, dribbling and/or rebounding being in a slightly bent position allows for easy movement. Standing straight up only wastes time, because in order to move you must bend down.

13 **Turnover.** *Perimeter/Post Dominate:* Teams and players tend to favor one area of the floor.

Steal. *Perimeter/Post Equality:* Distribute the ball to both areas of the floors equally. Balance the offense.

Example: When passing around the perimeter make a rule that every third pass should touch a post player's hands. If passing high to low post, make sure a pass reaches the perimeter every few passes.

14 **Turnover.** *Blindness:* Players who don't use the backboard when shooting at an angle and around the basket.

Steal. *Corrected 20/20 Vision:* Make use of the backboard when shooting at an angle and around the basket.

Example: Get in the habit of using the backboard to help improve shooting percentage and finishing the shot.

15 **Turnover.** *Succumbing to Screens:* Allowing a screen to be set.
Steal. *No Screens:* Don't allow the screen to be set and give up once it is.

Example: When playing defense try and not allow the offense to set a screen. If they do, execute your team's philosophy and don't fight through chest-to-chest, giving up once contact is made.

16 **Turnover.** *Letting Mistakes Dominate:* Giving up on the play after a mistake is made.
Steal. *Dominating Mistakes:* Develop the attitude of risk-taking toward mistakes. Don't give up because of a brief failure.

Example: When a bad pass is thrown and the opponent steals the ball, get back on defense instead of sulking about it.

17 **Turnover.** *Tangibles:* Anybody can shoot, dribble and pass.
Steal. *Intangible:* Do the small things that make a big difference on both the offensive and defensive ends of the floor.

18 **Turnover.** *Poor Shot, Pass and Dribble Selection:* Using poor judgment and forcing shots, passes and dribbling.
Steal. *Smart Shot, Pass and Dribble Selection:* Knowing the location, game situation and what is going on during the game is crucial.

Example: If the team is up five up with 10 seconds left in the game, there is no need to shoot a 3-point shot, pass to a teammate who is double teamed or dribble through traffic to the basket.

19 **Turnover.** *1-2-3-4-5 Numbering Player's System:* Players have become so used to what number they are labeled that they try to develop their game according to it.

Steal. *Just Being a Basketball Player:* Develop a game that is conducive to all positions on the floor. Practice drills/skills that with help improve the total game.

Example: If you only practice shooting from the perimeter because of the 2 label, then you will be hard-pressed to drive to the basket, post up if necessary or run the team.

20 **Turnover.** *Poor Stretching:* Just going through the motions when warming up and stretching.

Steal. *Smart Stretching:* Go through the whole routine before and after workouts.

Example: Avoid doing just one stretch for a short period of time. Do a few different stretches, 3 times for each body part and use a 10-second count as a standard.

Coach Stephanie V. Gaitley
Long Island University
Brooklyn, NY

Team Playbook: The Mental Game

Exercises for Getting to Know Your Players and Developing Team Chemistry

A great deal of our team's success has to do with our commitment to our players off the court. We want to know what they think and how they feel. This information is critical in developing the makeup of our team. We feel it is important to know our players' strengths and weaknesses both on the court and off. If the players realize that you are committed to them as people, they will be more committed to you as well.

Blackbird Hoop Question of the Day:

It is 1:00 a.m. You are on your way back to school and your car breaks down. We have practice at 7:00 a.m. List the player you would call first, second, third, etc. (Note: Each player has an equal opportunity to help you.)

1. _____

2. _____

3. _____

4. _____

5. _____

6. _____

7. _____

8. _____

9. _____

10. _____

11. _____

12. _____

13. _____

⇨ This exercise gives us an opportunity to see who they rely on off the court. Are there similarities to whom they rely on when on the court?

Blackbird Hoop Question of the Day:

You are on your way to the playground to play a game of pickup. Which four of your teammates do you take with you?

1._____

2._____

3._____

4._____

Why?

⇨ This exercise allows us the opportunity to see who the players want to play with and why.

Team Inquiry: "Getting to Know Me"

A. Family

B. Stengths

C. Weaknesses

D. What would you like people to know about you?

⇨ We use this exercise to quiz teammates on how well they know
   each other. We feel it is critical to our success that we are all committed to each other in order to be committed to a common goal.

Team Inquiry: "Who am I?"

1. What do you like most about yourself?

2. What do you like least about yourself?

3. What one person do you trust the most?

4. Who do you turn to when you need help?

5. What is your favorite part of basketball?

6. What part of practice do you dislike? Why?

7. What would you do differently if you were the head coach?

8. What do you want to do following graduation?

9. What is your purpose in life?

⇨ This exercise gives you an opportunity to find out more about your players. This is highly important when developing team chemistry.

Team Inquiry: "Knowing Our Roles"

Please list the top three in each category.

Rebounding:

    A. Offensive

        1. _____

        2. _____

        3. _____

    B. Defensive

        1. _____

        2. _____

        3. _____

Foul Shooting:

        1. _____

        2. _____

        3. _____

Three-Point Shooting:

        1. _____

        2. _____

        3. _____

Defense:

    A. On the Ball

        1. _____

        2. _____

        3. _____

B. Off the Ball (help)

1. _____

2. _____

3. _____

Leaders:

1. _____

2. _____

3. _____

Most Likely to Draw a Foul:

1. _____

2. _____

3. _____

Competitors:

1. _____

2. _____

3. _____

Abilty to Drive to the Basket:

1. _____

2. _____

3. _____

Players You Can Count on, Regardless of the Score:

1. _____

2. _____

3. _____

⇨ This exercise gives us an opportunity to see if the players think the same way that the coaches think. We all need to be on the same page come game time.

Coach Royce Chadwick
Marshall University
Huntington, West Virginia

Using a Video Grading System

Throughout my coaching career, we have used this grade sheet to break down our team defense and offense. It has been very good to us as we have identified players' strengths and weaknesses with this system. It allows us to play our strengths while we work on developing our weaknesses.

The original grade sheet was much more simple. Due to our Run and Jump defense, we have added additional categories. If you believe strongly in zones, you will need to adjust our categories. This sheet is our standard, but could be altered to custom fit any program.

The basic postivies and negatives are as follows:

POSITIVES

1. Great motivational tool
2. Tanglible, on-paper grades
3. Cut and dried for players, parents and personnel
4. Points out strengths
5. Points out deficiencies
6. Aids in picking starting players
7. Develops consistency with play

NEGATIVES

1. Takes time
2. Good video person is imperative
3. Does not measure everything happening on the court

The grades are determined by a series of positives and negatives. We try to set our own players up to have a positive score by making many positive categories worth more than one point, while the negative categories (except turnovers) are all only worth one point.

Breakdown

Positive Categories

Defensive Help (+2): In our help side defensive philosophy, any player who helps out a beaten teammate by leaving and stopping a driving player.

Offensive Rebound (+2): When a team rebound occurs, I give the credit to the player who was working to get the board as it was deflected out-of-bounds, or tied up, etc.

Defensive Rebound (+2): same as offensive rebound.

Assist (+2)

Steals (+2)

Taking a Charge (+3): The only three-point nonscoring opportunity.

Basket Made (+2): Can be a +3 if a 3-pointer is made.

Blocked Shot (+3)

Free Throws Made (+1): Possibly should be +2 or +3 as poorly as some percentages appear.

Loose Ball Recovery (+1): The steal goes to the player who deflects the ball or creates the loose ball opportunity. This category is for the player who actually ends up with the loose ball.

Positive Categories (cont.)

Screen/Basket (+1): The player who sets a screen which leads to a basket.

Hustle (+1): Dive on the floor, dive out-of-bounds.

Deflection (+1): On defense, deflecting a pass or dribble that does not result in a steal.

Scoring-Area Pass Made (+1): A pass that should have been an assist, but the basket was missed.

Transition Pass Ahead (+1): A pass up the floor to create our fast break.

> Analysis of a team and players is often one of the most difficult tasks we face. This grading system can be very useful in breaking down potential problem areas.

Negative Categories

Turnovers (-2): The only negative which is valued -2.

Not Rotating Full Court(-1): Our run and jump defense requires reading and rotating. Failure here results in a -1.

Missed Shot, First Half (-1)

Missed Shot, Second Half (-1): Two boxes ensure that there is enough space for all marks.

Missed Free Throw (-1)

Not Back on Defense (-1): The player's opponent beats her down the floor.

Scoring Area Pass (-1): The player that is being guarded by your player caught the ball in an area in which she should have scored.

Deflected Pass (-1): A pass which your player made was deflected, but did not result in a turnover.

Beaten on a Screen (-1): Improper defensive guarding of a screen situation.

Not Having Hands Up (-1): Especially for zone coaches.

Not Contesting the Shot (-1): Each shot by our opponent should be
taken with our player's hands high in the sight line.

Negative Categories (cont.)

Not Blocking Out (-1): Your player was not blocked off the board.

Not Overplaying (-1): Ballside players without the ball should be denied.

Influence Cut Off Baseline (-1): We influence the baseline. Any player who gets beat off the dribble to the middle or allows the ball handler to penetrate the paint-area baseline.

Not Going to the Boards (-1): Offensive rebounders who do not crash...HARD.

Not Helping in the Halfcourt (-1): Help-side players who fail to rotate over and stop penetrating dribblers in half-court sets.

"0" Execution Lapse (-1): Poor execution on offense.

No Ball Pressure (-1): Lack of defensive pressure on a dribbler, passer or dead player.

Defensive Lapse (-1): Anything on defense we want to emphasize for the day (slide step, hands on ball, see ball - see player, stance, etc.)

Offensive Lapse (-1): Failure to run the offensive set.

GRADE SHEET

		Player #1	Player #2	Player #3	Player #4	Player #5	Player #6	Player #7	Player #8	Player #9	Player #10	Player #11	
Defensive Help	+2												+2
Offensive Rebounds	+2												+2
Assists	+2												+2
Steals	+2												+2
Taking a Charge	+3												+3
Baskets Made	+2												+2
Blocked Shots	+2												+2
Free Throws Made	+1												+1
Loose Ball Recovery	+1												+1
Screen/Basket	+1												+1
Hustle	+1												+1
Deflection	+1												+1
Scoring Area Pass Made	+1												+1
Transition Pass Ahead	+1												+1
Positive Points	+1												+1
Turnovers	-2												-2
Not Rotating f(c)	-1												-1
Missed Shots/First Half	-1												-1
Missed Shots/Second Half	-1												-1
Missed Free Throw	-1												-1
Not Back on Defense	-1												-1
Scoring Area Pass Allowed	-1												-1
Deflected Pass	-1												-1
Beaten on Screen	-1												-1
Not Having Hands Up	-1												-1
Not Contesting Shot	-1												-1
Not Blocking Out	-1												-1
Not Overplaying	-1												-1
Influencing Cut Off	-1												-1
Not Going to the Boards	-1												-1
Not Helping Half-court	-1												-1
"0" Execution Lapse	-1												-1
No Ball Pressure	-1												-1
Defensive Lapse	-1												-1
Offensive Lapse	-1												-1
Negative Points	-1												-1
Game Totals													
Game #2													
Game #3													
CUMULATIVE TOTALS													

Tom Weaver, Former Coach
Albany College of Pharmacy
Albany, New York

Foul-Shot Golf

Purpose:

This drill is a fun way to practice shooting free throws.

Organization:

The players play 18 "holes" by rotating to different baskets in our gym. Each basket is a par-2 with a maximum of five attempts. Score is kept on cards obtained from a miniature golf course. The winner gets to sit out line drills, slides or foot fires at the next practice.

Coaching Notes:

♦ Replace all divots.

♦ Do not attempt to play out of sand traps.

♦ Our best free-throw shooter has been consistently scoring -9.

Hole	Par				
1	2				
2	2				
3	2				
4	2				
5	2				
6	2				
7	2				
8	2				
9	2				
10	2				
11	2				
12	2				
13	2				
14	2				
15	2				
16	2				
17	2				
18	2				
Total	36				

Coach Sue Semrau
Florida State University
Tallahassee, Florida

"Baseball" as a Basketball Drill

Purpose:
The objective of this drill is to learn how to work hard and have fun simultaneously.

Organization:
Two teams are formed and four players participate from each team at one time. The extras wait their turn on the baseline. The setting is four-on-four in the half court. The coach designates a number of "innings" that will be played. Generally, a three inning game fits well into practice time.

1) The team that starts with the ball on offense scores a point or a "run" for each basket. The offense works within the boundaries set by the coach. They remain on offense until the defense gets three stops or "outs." A stop consists of a steal or a defensive rebound.

2) When the defense gets a stop, the offense will start play again from the top of the key with one out in the inning. Defense cannot score runs, but works for three outs. After three outs, the offense and defense turn over and substitutions are made. At this point, one half of the inning has been completed. Once each team has an opportunity to play offense, one inning is complete.

Coaching Points:
Scoring may be altered to meet specific needs of practice. For example, three deflections during a defensive series can constitute one

out. In other words, during the course of an inning, if the defense deflects the ball, pass, blocked shot, or dribble off of the floor, play does not stop, but a deflection is scored. On the third deflection, play is stopped and an out is awarded to the defending team. Runs can be awarded based on different emphases of practice.

Meet the Coaches

Bill Agronin was the head women's coach at Niagara University for nine seasons. He posted a 32-22 record and back-to-back winning seasons during his first tenure and led the Purple Eagles to a first-place MAAC regular-season finish in 1992-93. Following the 1992-93 campaign, he was named MAAC Coach of the Year. In 2003, Agronin stepped down from the head coach position to assume to title of Associate Director of Athletics.

For the last 12 years, **Kevin L. Allen** has served as the head girls' varsity coach at West Florence High School in Florence, South Carolina, and a counselor at the Five-Star camp for the last eight years. Allen has been teaching and coaching for 22 years and has recently earned his master's degree in sports sciences at the United States Sports Academy.

With over a decade of playing and coaching in the Northeast Conference, Mount St. Mary's head women's basketball coach **Vanessa Blair** has emerged as one of the most notable figures in NEC women's basketball history. Garnering two NEC Player of the Year awards, NEC Player of the Decade and NEC Coach of the Year, Blair holds three of the highest honors given to a player or coach in the NEC. Proven by her résumé, Blair has continuously raised the bar for the Mount women's basketball program, showing the way for the Mount to reach higher heights.

Matt Brzycki is the Coordinator of Health Fitness, Strength and Conditioning Programs at Princeton University. He has authored several books and written more than 200 articles on strength and fitness for 34 different publications.

In eight seasons at Cleveland State University, **Duffy Burns** compiled an overall record of 101-121 (.455), including a 55-64 (.462) mark in league play. A member of the Women's Basketball Coaches Association Board of Directors, Burns' win total stands second in school history to only Alice Khol, who compiled 115 victories from 1980-91. In addition, he guided the Vikings to the 2000 conference championship finals — the only title game appearance in the 29-year history of the program.

Before becoming the head coach at Marshall University, **Royce Chadwick** spent seven seasons as head coach at Stephen F. Austin University, where his teams were known as fast, athletic, pressure-defense oriented type teams. He established himself as one of the top collegiate coaches in the nation based on wins. During his tenure at SFA, Chadwick averaged 24.7 wins per season (79.7%) and led the Ladyjacks to seven consecutive appearances in the NCAA Tournament.

Assistant Coach **Kevin Chaney** has been at Solano Community College since 1994. His duties have included everything from administration to on-court instruction.

Success is something that Auburn head coach **Joe Ciampi** has enjoyed throughout his career on the sideline. For 23 seasons at Auburn and two at West Point, Ciampi has never had a losing season. That success even came with him from his days of coaching high school. He has always won more games than he has lost. In his 23 years at the helm of the Tigers, Ciampi has won nearly three-quarters of his games, compiling a 523-184 (.740) record. He won his 500th game at Auburn on December 17, 2000 by defeating Puerto Rico-Mayaguez 106-25, making him the 13th coach to record 500 wins at one school. His overall record of 563-194 (.744) rates him as the 10th-winningest active division I coach in winning percentage and 10th among active division I coaches in wins.

Greg Collins is entering his second year as an assistant coach with the University of Louisville. His primary duties include player development, scouting opponents, recruiting and assisting with strength and conditioning. Collins joins Louisville after serving as an assistant athletic director and a varsity assistant coach at DuPont Manual High

School with head coach Mina Todd. While at Manual, the Lady Crimsons advanced to the state semifinals in 2000, finished as runner-ups in the 2001 Kentucky State Championship, and sent 13 players to play college basketball over a five-year period. From 2000-2002, he was the head coach of the Derek Smith All-Stars AAU team, featuring Kentucky's best prep stars. In 1998 Collins coached Manual to an AAU state championship. Coach Collins previously coached at North Bullitt High (Shepherdsville, Kentucky), where he started the North Bullitt Swoosh AAU program, leading them to their first National AAU Tournament in 1997.

Jody Conradt's long-term commitment to the sport has been recognized as a key factor in elevating women's basketball into the national spotlight. A four-time National Coach of the Year honoree, when UT defeated Texas Tech, 69-58 on January 22, 2003, Conradt joined an exclusive club — the 800 win club, joining Tennesse's Pat Summitt as the only women's coaches in history to win 800 games. Upon her 800th victory, Conradt had a 682-200 record in 276 seasons at Texas and ranked third in all-time wins behind Mount St. Mary's Jim Phelan and Summitt. She currently ranks as the all-time winningest women's basketball coach.

The head coach at Oglethorpe University in Atlanta, Georgia, **Kathy Warner Corbett** played college basketball for four years and graduated from Rollins College in Orlando, Florida. She has served as an assistant coach at both Furman University in Greenville, South Carolina, (where she also earned her master's degree), and Wright State University in Dayton, Ohio.

Coach **Paul Culpo** is a native of Pittsfield, Mass., and is in his second season under Coach Steve Lappas' at UMass, Amherst. Culpo, who has nine years of coaching experience on his résumé, spent the 2000-2001 season as the head coach and director of operations for England's Doncaster Panthers of the National Basketball League. He took a team picked to finish last by the media and coaches, to the playoffs in his only season there. Before that move, Culpo served as an assistant basketball coach at St. Michael's College (1997-2000), Union College (1996-1997), Genesee Community College (1995-1996) and UMass-Boston (1993-1995). A 1993 graduate of St. Michael's College, Culpo received his master's degree from UMass-Boston in 1996. He and his wife, Katy reside in Hadley with their children, Jac and Theresa.

Hired by Purdue on April 2, 1999, **Kristy Curry** was first blessed by being born into a coaching family. Her grandfather, Major Sims, was a teacher and coach for 41 years. Her father, Blake Sims, coached football in the prep ranks, and her mother, Ann Sims, coached girls basketball for 26 years. Curry, the first coach in NCAA women's basketball history to inherit a national champion team, made an impact in her first year with the Boilermakers. Despite beginning the 1999-2000 season ranked 23rd by the Associated Press (the lowest ever ranking for a defending NCAA champion), Curry engineered an impressive season by leading the Old Gold and Black to a 23-8 record (11-5 Big Ten), a third consecutive Big Ten Tournament championship, a top 16 seed in the NCAA Tournament and a final national ranking of 13th in the AP poll. Curry came to Purdue following three years as an assistant coach at Louisiana Tech under the legendary Leon Barmore.

Charlene Curtis has been the head coach at Wake Forest since 1997. She came to the Demon Deacons from the University of Connecticut, where she served as an assistant coach for two seasons under head coach Geno Auriemma. In that time, Curtis helped lead the Huskies to a combined 67-5 record and two Big East Conference championships. Her coaching résumé also includes a wealth of international experience. She was an assistant coach with the USA Basketball team that won a gold medal at the 1994 Goodwill Games, a bronze at the 1994 World Championships and a gold at the 1991 World University Games. She was a also a floor coach for the USA Basketball Olympic Trials in 1992.

June Daugherty, who has more than a decade of head coaching experience, entered the 2002-03 season with a 13-year career record of 223-152. Her first two victories of the 2002 season made her the second-winningest coach at the University of Washington. Washington's success on the court can be directly attributed to its team chemistry away from the basketball court. Daugherty, whose husband, Mike, is on her staff, is a firm believer in the "Husky Family" and creating a home away from home for her players and staff. The Daugherty twins, eight-year old Doc and Breanne, have grown up with Husky basketball. They are regulars on the travel squad and are often credited with an assist in recruiting.

In four short years, head coach **Cheryl Dozier** has earned respect for the University at Buffalo women's basketball program in the Mid-American Conference and in the regional ranks. Dozier has guided the Bulls to two record-setting starts, has seen her team receive votes in the Associated Press Top 25 poll and led last season's squad to a national ranking in two defensive statistical categories while also picking up her 60th career victory.

Bob Foley has coached boys and girls at every level over the past 30 years. The previous 24 years have been spent coaching at the Division I College level where he has won over 400 games and been involved in 10 NCAA tournaments. His coaching stops before coming to the University of Richmond, were at Providence College, Penn State, and Colorado. .

University of Maryland head coach **Brenda Oldfield Frese** has received high praise and numerous accolades during her young coaching career. People have described the 32-year-old head coach as dynamic, overachieving, determined and enthusiastic. The 2002 Associated Press National Coach of the Year, Frese has been a head coach for only three seasons, accumulating an astounding 57-30 (.655) record, while making amazing turnarounds her calling card. One of college basketball's rising stars, Frese fits with Maryland's legacy of success. At Minnesota, she earned AP National Coach of the Year honors as well as Big Ten Coach of the Year recognition for turning the Gopher's 8-20 program into a 22-8 Top 25 contender. One of the biggest one-season turnarounds in NCAA history, Minnesota set a school record with 22 wins and tied for second in the Big Ten with an 11-5 conference mark. Frese also took the Gophers to what was only the school's second NCAA appearance.

Stephanie Gaitley's name has become one of the more recognized in college basketball with a 312-151 career record, seven NCAA Tournament berths, four conference championships and two WNIT appearances. Gaitley sported a 196-88 mark in 10 seasons at St. Joseph's University (1991-2001) and went 116-63 in six seasons at the University of Richmond (1985-91). She was named the head coach at Long Island University in the fall of 2002.

In 2002, **David Glass** began his seventh season as coach of Virginia Commonwealth's women's basketball team, the longest tenure in the program's history. During his stint at VCU, Glass has recorded an overall record of 83-87. A 1986 graduate of Virginia Commonwealth, Glass returned to VCU in 1996 after serving as the head coach at the University of Missouri-Kansas City from 1993-96. Since Glass' return in 1996, the Rams have appeared in the Colonial Athletic Association tournament semifinals three times while finishing in the top-five in the conference four times.

Allison Greene led Dartmouth to four consecutive Ivy League conference championships in the late 80's. An All-Ivy League selection during her last two seasons, Greene played 103 career games and still ranks among the leaders in career statistics for scoring, rebounding, and assists. Upon graduation, Greene went overseas to play for the Portugal National team (at the time, no women's professional basketball leagues existed in the U.S.). Her team went on to win three national championships. After a very successful stint as an assistant coach with Old Dominion, Greene is now working on her dissertation in the Towson, Md. area.

Former Hawk standout **Cindy Anderson Griffin** entered her second year as head coach of the Saint Joseph's University women's basketball team in 2002. A 1991 graduate of SJU, Griffin was named the seventh head coach in the program's 29-year history on April 25, 2001. She previously served as the head women's basketball coach at Loyola College from 1999-2001. In her first year at her alma mater, Griffin helped to reinvigorate the SJU program, leading the squad to a 24-8 record and the second round of the WNIT. She capitalized on the team's tradition of scrappy play and rugged defense, while releasing the reins and allowing the team to play a more up-tempo style on the offensive end of the floor. The Hawks finished the year among the national leaders in nine different categories and paced the nation in free-throw shooting accuracy for the second straight year.

Karen Hall was formerly the head coach at North Carolina Agricultural and Technical State University. In 1994 Hall was hired by Chatham College in Pittsburgh to initiate, develop and be head coach of the school's first NCAA women's basketball program. Hall, who

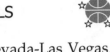

played basketball collegiately at the University of Nevada-Las Vegas, served as an assistant coach at Cleveland State (1992-93) and at Duquesne (1989-91). An All-Pacific Coast Athletic Association performer and two-time team captain while at UNLV, she became the first woman to play and coach in the Connie Hawkins Men's Summer League and was the first woman to coach at Five-Star national boys summer basketball camp.

Since coming to the University of North Carolina at Chapel Hill in 1986, **Sylvia Hatchell** has posted a record of 269-133 and forged a tradition of excellence. Under her direction, the Tar Heels have won a national championship, four of the last six ACC titles, compiled back-to-back 30-win seasons, and claimed four ACC Player of the Year and three ACC Rookie of the Year honors. With a 33-2 record in 1993-94 and a 30-5 record in 1994-95, Hatchell became the first UNC basketball coach, men's or women's, to post back-to-back 30-win seasons. In 1994, Hatchell was named the National Coach of the Year by *USA Today* and *College Sports* magazine. In 1996-97, she was named ACC Coach of the Year after guiding the Tar Heels to a 15-1 conference record and their first regular-season ACC title. Hatchell's stints in international competition also include serving as an assistant coach for the U.S. World University Games team that won the gold medal in 1983 and the team that won a silver medal in 1985. She was a court coach at the U.S. Olympic basketball tryouts in both 1984 and 1992 and also worked on the Olympic Games basketball events staff in Los Angeles in 1984. In her initial task for the Amateur Basketball Association of the United States of America, she coached the South team to the gold medal at the 1982 National Sports Festival.

In six years as the head mentor at Virginia Tech, **Bonnie Henrickson** has led the Hokies to a 113-43 record, three trips to the NCAA Tournament and two WNIT appearances. Henrickson's 2001-02 team became the eighth 20-plus win team in Hokie history and her fifth straight as the Virginia Tech head coach.

When speaking about **Keith Holubesko**, the word "teacher" is the first thing that comes to mind. Priding himself on his ability to create the perfect drill for any skill situation, Coach Holubesko started his coaching career as an assistant girls' coach at Bridgewater State College in

Massachusetts from 1994-97. In 1998, Coach Holubesko took over as head girls' basketball coach at Rogers High School in Newport, Rhode Island and then went to work for the Five-Star Basketball Camps full-time in 2002.

John Ishee has been a women's coach and strong recruiter for more than 14 years at the high school and collegiate levels. He is currently at Life University in Marietta, Georgia.

Craig Kennedy is an assistant coach for the Tigers women's basketball program. He was promoted after serving one season as the director of basketball operations at Auburn. Kennedy came to Auburn after a four-year stint as the head girl's and boy's basketball coach at Lee-Scott Academy in Auburn. At Lee-Scott he led the boy's program to three straight elite eight appearances, including a trip to the state final four in 1998. Prior to his time at Lee-Scott, Kennedy served an assistant coach and interim head coach of the University of Winnipeg women's program from 1988 to 1995. During his stay at Winnipeg he led his team to 20 victories and a top 10 national ranking in 1995 as interim head coach.

Coach **Elizabeth Lawson** has been a resident coach and counselor at Ron DeCarli's Girls' Basketball Camp from 1997 through 2000 and in 2002. She also began working at Five-Star Basketball Girls' Camp in 1999, serving as counselor and resident coach for the past four years. In 2001, Coach Lawson took over as the head varsity girls' basketball coach at Clinton Christian School in Upper Marlboro, Maryland, where she is a physical education and health teacher.

Nancy Lieberman continues her role as a broadcaster for ESPN covering the Women's NCAA championships and WNBA games. She also coaches young women's basketball camps in Dallas, during the summer. Her basketball camps focus on basketball fundamentals, drug awareness, confidence, self-esteem and the secrets to winning. Nancy also speaks to Fortune 500 companies and high school banquets. Nancy Lieberman also dedicates herself to many local and national charities such as the Girl Scouts of America, The Childhood Diabetes Foundation, Jimmy V Foundation and Special Olympics.

Matt Masiero is co-editor for the new Five-Star books *My Favorite Moves: Shooting Like the Stars* and *Making the Big Plays,* which feature 12

WNBA Players. Matt began working for the Five-Star Basketball Camp in 1993. For the past 10 years, his duties have included serving as a counselor and resident coach, head counselor, commissioner, and most recently, junior camp director. In 1998, Coach Masiero took over as director of the women's camp (at Robert Morris University) and has helped lead the camp to their highest enrollment over its 23 year existence, while employing some of the best women coaches in the game. Coach Maserio has also assisted Tamika Catchings, with her "Catch the Fever" Basketball Camps, in Indianapolis. He is also the former UMass Boston associate men's basketball and head girls' basketball coach at Jeremiah E. Burke High School.

A.C. McCullers, the third-winningest girls' basketball coach in Georgia after a legendary career at Morrow High School, is the fourth head women's basketball coach in Clayton College & State University history. The most successful coach in Clayton County history, McCullers compiled a career record of 648-157, a winning percentage of .803, and won 535 games at Morrow before announcing his retirement in the spring of 1999. He led the Lady Mustangs to Class AAAA state championships in 1989, 1990, 1991 and 1993 and had nine players sign with NCAA Division I programs since 1990. In 25 years, McCullers guided Morrow to 19 state tournament appearances, 12 regional championships and nine trips to the Final Four, including his last season.

Joe McKeown came to George Washington University in mid-September of 1989, inheriting a team that went 9-19 a year earlier. In just 14 months, McKeown had built the Colonials into one of the elite programs in the country. His first team improved five games, to a 14-14 record, and the program has soared past the .500 mark since then. In 1991, he was named an "All-American Coach" by the American Women's Sports Federation after being chosen the Atlantic 10 Coach of the Year. McKeown has also produced winning teams off the court, in the classroom. His philosophy of the student-athlete balance has made well-rounded people out of the players he has coached. During McKeown's tenure, the Colonials have not only produced All-Conference winners on the court, but Academic All-America and Academic All-Conference winners in the classroom. Under McKeown's tutelage, the Colonials have received Atlantic 10 Academic All-Conference recognition 14 times.

One of the goals of head coach **Cristy McKinney** when she arrived at Rice 10 years ago was to take a program that was a perennial cellar-dweller and make winning the expectation, not the exception. Nine years later, McKinney has more than succeeded in her goal with her Lady Owls producing six consecutive winning seasons, including four seasons with 20 or more victories. For the 24 years for which records exist, McKinney's teams have produced more than 46 percent of the Rice victories and more than 58 percent of the Lady Owls' wins since first playing in the NCAA in the 1982-83 season. Touted as one of the best overall teachers of the game, McKinney guided the Rice women to four of their best seasons ever in 1998 (21-9), 1999 (20-12), 2000 (22-10) and 2002 (21-9). She has posted an overall record of 155-107 in nine seasons with the Lady Owls.

A 1986 graduate of Northern Illinois University, **Jack Miller** has been an assistant coach and recruiting coordinator at Rider University since 1999. Before arriving at Rider, Miller was an assistant coach at Monmouth University from 1991-1999 and served as an assistant at Seton Hall University. Before entering the college ranks, Miller was the head girls' basketball coach at Elgin St. Edward high school. In his first season, he led the Lady Wave to a 25-7 record and a fourth place finish in the 1991 Illinois Class A state tournament. Miller has been teaching and coaching for the past 15 years and received his Masters in Education in 1994.

Coach **Mariana O'Connor** first began her coaching career at the collegiate level, where she was an assistant women's coach at Division III, UMass Boston. Coach O'Connor began working for the Five-Star in 1999, as a resident coach for the first ever Five-Star Women's Basketball Jamboree. She then took her teaching talents (and players) to Robert Morris University, where she became one of Five-Star's brightest young coaches. Mariana is currently the head girls' coach at Latin Academy High School in Boston, where she has led the Lady Dragons to a Boston City Championship second place finish and numerous MIAA tournament appearances. She is the former assistant coach from Boston Latin High School, where she was a high school standout. Mariana also played her collegiate ball as a walk-on at Northeastern University in Boston.

Dave Odom, who guided Wake Forest's women's team to nine consecutive post-season appearances, including seven straight NCAA
Tournament trips from 1991 through 1997, and Atlantic Coast Conference championships in 1995 and 1996, is recognized as one of the
premier collegiate basketball coaches in America. Three times he has
been chosen district coach of the year by the U.S. Basketball Writers
Association and twice he has been a National Association of Basketball
Coaches award-winner on the district level as well. The Touchdown
Club of Columbus also named him its 1995 national coach-of-the-year
after conducting a poll of head coaches across the country. In 2002
Coach Odom became the head men's coach at South Carolina.

At the professional or collegiate level, as a player or coach, **Belinda
"Boe" Pearman** knows the meaning of success. Pearman, who is the
fifth head women's basketball coach in Rhode Island's history, spent
the past two seasons with American Basketball League's most popular
franchise, the New England Blizzard, first as an assistant then as associate head coach. Pearman's innovative schemes allowed the Blizzard,
who led the ABL in attendance in her two seasons with the club, to
evolve from a league doormat to a very competitive squad. In
Pearman's first season, New England climbed out of the Eastern
Division's cellar into the playoffs after posting a 24-20 record and a
second-place finish.

For the past 13 years, **Kevin Pigott** has been the head varsity basketball coach at Fordham Preparatory School in the Bronx. Fordham Prep
plays in the powerful New York City Catholic High School League.
Coach Pigott has been an assistant coach at All Hallows in the Bronx
and Bishop Guertin in Nashua, New Hampshire. He has a record at
Fordham of 172 varsity wins and 148 varsity loses.

A veteran of 15 years in the collegiate ranks as a player, assistant coach
and head coach, **Jill Pizzotti** entered her sixth season at the helm at
Saint Louis University in 2002. Pizzotti came to Saint Louis University
from Indiana University, where she served as assistant coach for three
seasons. She was the Hoosiers' recruiting coordinator and worked
closely with Indiana's post players. Pizzotti has compiled 45 wins in
fours seasons after taking over a program that hadn't won that many in
the previous eight seasons combined. She has a 45-64 mark at the

university in her first collegiate head coaching position. Pizzotti is already the second-winningest coach in school history.

Hired in 1997 to be head coach at Manhattanville College, **Stephen Post** had the benefit of more than 20 years of coaching experience. He won three New York City high school championships and three New York City High School Coach of the Year awards. He has also served as an assistant coach at Division I Iona and Manhattan Colleges.

Cheryl Reeve was the head coach at Indiana State University for five years before joining the coaching staff of the Charlotte Sting.

When you think of a standout Boston high school and college basketball player, **John "Boo" Rice's** name comes to mind. After Boston State College closed in 1982, Coach Rice transferred to Division III powerhouse UMass Boston for the 1982-1983 season. He quickly earned Division III All-American honors and became the only male basketball player to have his jersey retired. He was later drafted by the Boston Celtics in the seventh round of the 1983 NBA draft.

Since the day she signed scholarship papers to play basketball at Ole Miss, University of Florida coach **J. Carol Ross** spent more than 20 years both creating and soaking up the traditions of arguably the finest women's basketball conference in the country. As a player at Ole Miss in the early 1980s, she was a member of the inaugural SEC All-Tournament Team. As a seven-year assistant coach at Auburn, Ross reached the NCAA championship game in each of her last three seasons — 1988, '89 and '90. Ross is Florida's all-time winningest coach, compiling a 184-91 record (66.9 winning percentage) in her first 10 years at the school.

Head women's basketball coach at SUNY Potsdam since 1999, **Nelson Schorr** was previously the assistant coach at SUNY Potsdam (1998-99) and Indian River (1995-98). Schorr is also the director of the Nelson Schorr 3-on-3 Charity Tournament and the basketball director at Camp Chen-A-Wanda. He has served as a lecturer at numerous camps and clinics throughout the Northeast.

Since arriving at Florida State five years ago, **Sue Semrau** has literally had to rebuild the women's basketball program from the ground up and her efforts have begun to pay dividends. Florida State had a breakout season in 2000-01 as Semrau guided the Seminoles to a No. 25 final ranking with a 19-12 record, a third-place finish in the ACC and its first NCAA Tournament since 1990-91. It was Florida State's first winning season since 1991-92 as well as the school's best league finish since joining the ACC in 1991. The Seminoles were the only team in the nation to defeat Duke on its home court in 2000-01. The Seminoles earned their highest-ever seed in the ACC Tourney at No. 4 and advanced to the tournament's semifinals for the first time. Her efforts were recognized and rewarded when the Atlantic Coast Sports Writers Association announced that Semrau was named the 2001 Atlantic Coast Conference Coach of the Year.

Coach **Tom Shirley** has been with Philadelphia University for 14 seasons. Shirley entered the 2002-2003 season as the ninth-winningest active women's coach in NCAA Division II. Shirley came to then-Philadelphia Textile in 1989 as both the head women's basketball coach and associate director of athletics. In January of 1992, he succeeded H.R. Ted Taylor as the university's director of athletics, a position he still holds.

Following three highly-successful years as head girls basketball coach at Bishop Hartley High School, **Jessica Smith** joined Miami University's women's basketball program as an assistant coach prior to the 2001-02 campaign. A 1995 graduate of Rhode Island, Smith served as a student-assistant coach with the Rams from 1992-95 and was hired as a full-time assistant for the 1995-96 season. During that season, Rhode Island made its first NCAA Tournament appearance while capturing a share of the Atlantic 10 Conference Championship. Smith spent the next two seasons as an assistant coach and recruiting coordinator at Fordham before accepting the reins at Bishop Hartley High School in Columbus, Ohio, in 1998.

Eric Stratman has been coaching in Quincy, Illinois, for the last six years. He won an eighth-grade girls' state championship before moving to the position of varsity girls' basketball coach at Quincy Senior High School in 1999. Stratman's team went 18-8, and he was named IBCA District 17 Coach of the Year. He and his wife Julie have a son, Alexander.

Debbie Taneyhill became the first CAA women's basketball player to advance to head coach at the same institution. At age 29, the head coach at George Mason University is also currently the youngest head women's basketball coach in Division I. Upon taking over the helm of the Patriots, Taneyhill promptly led her squad to three straight victories over Maryland-Eastern Shore, UNC Wilmington and East Carolina. George Mason would then go on to sweep series with UNCW, ECU and William & Mary. Last season Taneyhill guided Mason to series sweeps over American, UNCW and VCU. Twice during the season they put together a string of three consecutive victories.

Coach **Roberto (Rob) Thompson** is a post player's post coach. At 28 years old, he has been coaching more than half his life and professes that he is "more organized than crime." For 15 years as either an assistant or head varsity coach; to coach and athletic director for the Tucson Hebrew Academy; to organizing, heading and running Tucson's only post camp, Coach Thompson never stops working to perfect his craft. Rob Thompson was invited to coach at Five-Star's first ever post camp in 1998 and has been coaching three or more sessions each summer since. He has combined passion for the game and deep understanding of footwork and fundamentals to make himself one of Five-Star Basketball Camps greatest teachers.

In a storied 23-year coaching career, **Tara VanDerveer** has established herself as one of the top coaches in the history of both collegiate and international women's basketball. In 16 years as the head coach of the Stanford women's basketball team, she is an amazing 396-105 (.790) and just four wins shy of the 400 mark. During her tenure on The Farm, she has led the Cardinal to two NCAA Championships, five NCAA Final Four appearances, 10 Pacific-10 conference titles and 15 consecutive appearances in the NCAA tournament. VanDerveer's enormous contributions to the sport were recognized in April of 2002 when she was inducted into the Women's Basketball Hall of Fame in Knoxville, Tennessee.

Following an exciting 10 year career at the University of Colorado, including a trip to the 2002 NCAA West Regional Final in Boise, Coach **Jen Warden** brought excitement and intensity to Boise State when she became head coach following the 2001-2002 season. On March 26, 2002,

Jen Warden was named head coach of the Broncos and was handed the responsibility of building Boise State into a WAC championship contender. In the 32-year history of the program Warden is the fifth head coach to lead the Broncos.

After coaching the Albany College of Pharmacy's women's soccer team for five seasons (1991-1995) with a 41-23-2 record, **Tom Weaver** took over the helm of the Lady Panther basketball team for several seasons.

Debra Wein, M.S., R.D. is the president and co-founder of The Sensible Nutrition Connection (www.sensiblenutrition.com), a consulting firm providing nutrition services to universities, corporate wellness programs, health clubs and other organizations. Debra is a contributing editor for IDEA's *Personal Trainer* and *Health and Fitness Source* magazines serving fitness and exercise professionals. She writes regularly for *Men's Health* magazine and has published articles in *Marie Clare, Women's Sports and Fitness* and *Muscle and Fitness*. She has also been quoted in publications such as *Shape, Self, Allure and Prevention*. Debra has been featured on a number of occasions on the Fox 25 (WFXT-Boston) news talking about soy, men's health, weight loss and many other nutrition and fitness-related topics. Debra has over 10 years of experience managing leading university fitness centers in New York and Boston. Debra is the author of *SNaC Pack: The Health Professional's Guide to Nutrition*.

One of the most admired and respected coaches on the international and collegiate basketball scene, Coach **Kay Yow** has amassed over 500 wins in her 24 years at the helm of the North Carolina State women's basketball program. Yow's squads have won four Atlantic Coach Conference championships and appeared in post-season tournaments 18 times. In 15 of the last 23 seasons, Wolfpack teams have won more than 20 games and appeared in the final Associated Press Top 20 poll. During her illustrious career, Yow has worked with two United States Olympic Teams and seven other U.S. select teams, including Pan American, World University and World Championship squads. In 1988, she guided the U.S. Olympic Team to a gold medal. Yow has received numerous awards and accolades such as the prestigious Carol Eckman Award, whose recipient is selected by members of the Women's Basketball Coaches Association. The award is presented to an active coach who best demonstrates sportsmanship, honesty, courage, ethical behavior, dedication to purpose and a commitment to the student athlete.

Index

305